A
Canary
in a Coal Mine

Hope for a Culture in Free Fall

Dr. John S. Powers

with

Charles Garner

A Canary in a Coal Mine

ISBN: 979-8-218-31948-9

Acknowledgements:

Bible Versions used in the Text:
Berean Study Bible
English Standard Version
Holman Christian Standard Bible
King James Version
New American Standard Bible 1977
New Revised Standard Version
Webster Bible Translation

Unless noted, Scripture references are from the English Standard Version.

Contributors:
We benefitted from the assistance of several contributors: Mike Arrington, Becky Burris, Reuel Cruce, Jimmy Draper, Ernest Easley, Jerry and Susan Ferguson, John Fuller, Linda Garner, Nancy Garner, Jon Gehman, Frank Harbour, Steve Kelly, James LaPierre, Malcolm McDow, David Michel, Matt Tacker, Michael Wells, and Hayes Wicker. With gratitude, we acknowledge their contribution to this work and to our nation.

About the Authors:

Dr. John Powers has been a professional writer for more than 25 years. His focus addresses leadership challenges in and among congregations. His works include: *The BodyLife Journey: Guiding Believers into Ministry* and *Redefining Church Membership* along with countless articles discussing leadership issues.

Dr. Powers has an undergraduate degree in economics as well as a Master of Divinity and Doctor of Ministry from Southwestern Baptist Theological Seminary. He has served churches in Tennessee, Texas, and Virginia.

Connie and he have one son and two grandchildren. The Powers reside in East Tennessee.

Charles Garner is an author, curriculum designer, and teacher to the church. His B.A. is in Biblical Studies and Social Science. He holds a Master of Religious Education with emphasis in Biblical Exegesis and Theology.

He has authored, edited, or designed over fifty resources and books for use in the Christian community. His works include *Gifts of Grace, Teaching to Make a Difference, Reclaiming the Real Jesus*, co-authored with Dr. Ivan Parke, and *Thinking of Leaving*.

He and his wife, Nancy, live in the Northern Rockies of Montana.

Contents

Note to the Reader:

A Canary in a Coal Mine deals with big issues—potential nation killers—from a historical, biblical/theological perspective. We set out principles of personal and national repentance. We urge you to educate yourself, to engage the fray, to enlist everyone possible to join you.

But be aware that events and circumstances are unfolding so rapidly that they should be on a streaming feed. At a point, we had to go to press to put this sentinel warning and call to action in your hands.

Please allow some grace to temper your perceptions. The principles, the history, the Scripture, and the theology do not change. The events that call for our attention and create diversions, however, are unfolding each day. Just staying informed is a challenge. Let the latest atrocities in the headlines be a further call to action.

In this edition, you will find extra pages in the front and back of the book. These are for notes, additional information, questions, and actions that you will take to impact the future of our nation.

The time to arouse from sleep is far past. Action is demanded. The trumpet has sounded. Respond to the call now.

The Publishers

Author's Note

2023 is a year I will *never* forget.

On a January morning one of my doctors announced, "Mr. Powers, I do not have good news." Initial chemotherapy treatments had been unsuccessful. "Mr. Powers, if the second round of treatments do not cure the leukemia, this is the extent of our ability to fight this kind of cancer."

I asked him, "If these treatments fail to perform, what is my life expectancy?"

With his eyes cast downward, he said, "Mr. Powers you will have *two months* to live."

We are all terminal. We all know that. But when the doctor tells you, "two months," suddenly, it gets real and very personal.

Staring death squarely in the face, I wondered about the future of my family: my wife of almost 50 years; my son and grandchildren; my businesses and other interests.

Alone in my hospital bed, thoughts turned from personal reflections to contemplating the kind of life I would be passing down to my son and grandchildren. I began thinking about our country. The America that had given me such freedom and opportunity was being erased by blatant wickedness. Waves of deep consternation washed over my heart. It was then I began to view the nation I love through another filter—what some call a "biblical worldview."

Feelings of anger, fear, and frustration about the moral condition of America clouded my vision. But the grace, mercy, and hope we have in Christ broke through like sunlight after the storm. It was also when the initial thoughts of *A Canary in a Coal Mine: Hope for a Culture in Freefall* began forming. Like prophets of the Old Testament, I felt divine pressure, a burden of sorts, to begin a journey that became a consuming mission.

The second round of chemotherapy was a glowing success. Fourteen days after being told "two months," I was clear. Released to go home, I was waiting for a bone marrow donor to be located.

The burden of our nation and its future lay heavily upon me still. God directed me in providing a biblical response to the moral free fall of America. That response, you are holding in your hand.

Our nation, our culture is on the precipice of an abyss. It's why I am calling, asking, and pleading that those of us who name Jesus as Lord awaken out of a spiritual stupor to fight the evil forces of darkness seeking to destroy our nation.

Six months after the initial diagnosis, I was in another hospital room receiving a bone marrow transplant from some unknown but compassionate donor. That treatment might give me an extension on this physical life. But I am still a dying man. We are all dying. We begin that process the moment we are born. Before we die, we should ask ourselves, "What will we leave behind?"

America faces dark times. But hope remains. An exciting future waits to be secured by today's believers in the Lord Jesus. It includes a legacy of strong spiritual underpinnings flowing from an abiding relationship with Him. Our hope is revival among God's people and spiritual awakening that spreads across America. May it be ushered in by proverbial canaries like you and me who fearlessly enter a cultural coal mine called America!

Dr. John Powers
Cleveland, Tennessee
September 9, 2023

[Editor's Note: Sadly, our friend, Dr. John Powers, died on October 9, 2023. We sorrow, but not without hope. John has left us a great and needed word to the church and to our nation.]

Foreword

"Politics is downstream from culture."
Andrew Breitbart

This quote by Andrew Breitbart explains why America is in the mess that it is in. *A Canary in a Coal Mine* is a call to action for Christians to get involved in the cultural war raging in America today.

Only by winning the "cultural war" can American Christians win the "political war." The relevant question for Americans concerned about where America is going is, "What is upstream from culture?" The answer is the nuclear family, the Church, and the schools. Only by recapturing these foundations of American culture can the political battle be won.

As an active participant in the political arena, I continually hear the refrain, "Why can't we just all get along." That mentality is a recipe for failure, because the opposition to traditional American culture and values isn't interested in tranquility or compatibility. They mean to "fundamentally transform America" in the words of former President, Barack Obama. And they are not going to accept anything except total victory.

As a long-time American Government and History teacher, I would begin every semester with the Declaration of Independence and a discussion of the purpose of government.

In general terms, the purpose of government is justice. The definition of justice is determined by those who participate in the government. Thomas Jefferson in the Declaration of Independence says, "to secure these rights (life, liberty and pursuit of happiness), governments are instituted among men."

Therefore, the logical conclusion is that in this self-governing system of government, only those who participate will have their rights protected. Too many Americans in recent times have been reluctant to stand firm for their beliefs and values in the face of mockery, name-calling, and "cancelling." Nobody likes being called a racist, homophobe, or intolerant fanatic.

The result has been that rather than fighting back, many Christians have withdrawn and conceded by their absence the political arena to the enemy. The progressive stereotype of the tyrannical, ignorant, evangelical Christian is false. The reality is that Christianity has been the heart of true social progress and major advancements in human liberty, equality, and democratic government.

A Canary in a Coal Mine is a siren call to action for those Christians tempted to insist they are "not of this world." It is a call to step forward boldly defending the Kingdom and, ultimately, America.

John Fuller
Montana State Senator

Preface

Have you ever had the dream where you had the sense of falling? For some it is a recurring nightmare. They awake in a cold sweat. Fear gripping them. Then they realize the nightmare was not real. But what if the nightmare was real? Not for that individual. But for our nation.

America is falling. We have the sense that things are not right. It matters not in which part of the country you live, you are aware of and are affected by an onslaught of enemies attacking the nation on every front. Consider just a few—

- The national debt
- The plague of illegal and legal drug addiction
- Homelessness
- Rising crime of every description
- Failure of prosecutors to hold, try, and judge criminals
- An invasion of the southern border
- Child and adult sex-trafficking
- Gender confusion and perversion
- War in Ukraine that threatens to ramp up into World War III
- The idolatry of AI
- Unrestricted war from China
- Insidious inflation and stagnant wages
- Fragmentation of the culture

And this is just a partial list off the top of our minds. It took only a matter of minutes to compose the list. How many more dangers could be added with just a little more thought?

America is 247 years old as of the printing of this work. The question is how much longer can we survive?

Our nation survived a Revolutionary War, a Civil War, World Wars I and II, the Korean and Vietnam conflicts, the Afghanistan and Iraq wars, and now the involvement in Ukraine and that is not to mention the conflicts and wars we have engaged like Granada, Kosovo, and others.

The rise of global terrorism pushed America into the Middle East where brave men and women stood tall for seven long years enduring blazing desert heat and then became embroiled in an Afghanistan conflict that painfully lasted for twenty years—to little or no avail. And now we are flirting with the possibility of another unending war in Eastern Europe (we've been there before). And just as we go to press, war has reignited in the Middle East as Israel has come under attack. Our military is assembling in the Mediterranean.

We have forgotten the admonition of our forefathers. As a refresher, here are some warnings George Washington gave the nation in his farewell address, Saturday, September 17, 1796:

About political parties:
"However [political parties] may now and then answer popular ends, they are likely in the course of time and things, to become potent engines, by which cunning, ambitious, and unprincipled men will be enabled to subvert the power of the people and to usurp for themselves the reins of government, destroying afterwards the very engines which have lifted them to unjust dominion."

About the public debt:
"As a very important source of strength and security, cherish public credit. One method of preserving it is to use it as sparingly as possible."

About foreign entanglements:
In his farewell address, Washington exhorted Americans to set aside

their violent likes and dislikes of foreign nations, lest they be controlled by their passions: "The nation which indulges toward another an habitual hatred or an habitual fondness is in some degree a slave." Washington's remarks have served as an inspiration for American isolationism, and his advice against joining a permanent alliance was heeded for more than a century and a half. *(Office of The Historian, State Department—https://history.state.gov/milestones/1784-1800/ washington-farewell)*

Add to these comments the far-sighted warnings in the farewell address of President Dwight D. Eisenhower:

"In the councils of government, we must guard against the acquisition of unwarranted influence, whether sought or unsought, by *the military-industrial complex*. The potential for the disastrous rise of misplaced power exists and will persist."

"Ike" was famous for warning of the military-industrial complex. Yet, in that same address he warned of money in politics and of a scientific-technological elite. He warned of the corruption and control of an elite oligarchy. What would he say of the situation we are facing today in the world? Here's what he said in 1961:

"The prospect of domination of the nation's scholars by Federal employment, project allocations, and *the power of money is ever present* and is gravely to be regarded."

"Yet, in holding scientific research and discovery in respect, as we should, we must also be alert to the equal and opposite danger that public policy could itself become the captive of a *scientific-technological elite*." *(https://www. archives.gov)*

Heed the Warnings
Today, our nation faces global obstacles and adversaries unlike any other time in our rich history. The talking heads of national media

outlets would have all of us believe there are no existential threats to our culture, our way of life, our very survival.

This might be one of the more controversial and sobering books you might find on the plight of our nation's future. Like a burr under a cowboy's saddle, our hope is that you are willing to become uncomfortable, stirred, and ready to make noticeable and necessary changes. It is *not* just a piece to inform you. It is a call to action. It is a call to hope.

To borrow a phrase, America is going to hell in a handbasket. Some of you might never have heard that phrase. It is of uncertain origin. But it indicates a situation in which something or someone is on a path headed for inescapable disaster. To a great extent America appears to be entering a death spiral. The current situation demands immediate action.

Your informed involvement makes a difference in the direction of our nation. Like a ship needs a rudder, the opportunity for course corrections is closing faster than we might realize. It was in his 1905 work entitled, *The Life of Reason* that George Santayana warned:

"Those who cannot remember the past are condemned to repeat it."

History is not cyclical. It is linear. That means, it's headed in a specific direction. However, the traveler who blindly treks into the future without a firm grasp on the past unfortunately forgets that history is driven by flawed human nature. How this world and our nation might be better off had Santayana's philosophy served as a guide in our public and private lives. The American culture is like a critically ill patient who lies on an emergency room gurney. We are in a fight for our lives. That's why this book exists today.

The goal of *A Canary in a Coal Mine: Hope for a Culture in Free Fall* is to awaken our nation, especially that segment of citizenry who have become discouraged, disenchanted, disengaged, or disinterested in the moral free fall of America. It's impossible to fathom that so many people who have a God-given voice choose to remain silent. What will you discover by reading this book? It begins by remembering the triad of warnings when approaching a railroad crossing:

STOP - When you are in a hole, stop digging. There might never have been a more important time to tap the brakes socially, morally, spiritually, economically, and politically than today. A clear call for stopping the insanity is the need for the day.

LOOK – Look around you. Do you like what you see? Common-sensed people would shout a resounding, "NO!" Americans have shouted "NO!" throughout her 247-year history. The Boston Tea Party, the attack on Pearl Harbor, and the Civil Rights Movement of the 1960's are but three pivotal gateposts of changes to our nation. It may be time for a 21st century populous movement, where a group of concerned citizens rise to declare, "ENOUGH!" A call for change is imperative.

LISTEN – The vast majority of us are guilty of turning a deaf ear to our culture in free fall. How many of us marginalize conversations in which we do not agree and therefore justify our reasoning for tuning out these voices? Today, our culture is facing critical choices. Just as our individual lives are the sum total of the decisions we have made, so too the nation's collective life is the sum of its decisions. And choices have consequences. Remember, our choices determine direction and direction determines destiny.

So we are clear, this book is written by Christian patriots. It is a call for our nation to return to the roots of her Judeo-Christian heritage. Hopefully, it will be a challenge against the insane decision making of Republicans and Democrats (who are opposite sides of the same worthless coin). Political parties have never been and will never be the answer to the ills of our nation. Remember George Washington's warning about political parties.

Before carefully reading *A Canary in a Coal Mine,* be mindful of these three imperatives:

- *Become informed because our culture is replete with generational "dumb down."*
- *Become inspired because our nation is too young to die.*
- *Become engaged by being a voice of reason midst the mindless chatter that surrounds us.*

You have been warned.

Do you remember playing the school yard game, "I dare you?" Then someone would say, "I double dare you?" The next response raised intensity of the moment saying, "I triple dare you?" The Mount Everest of all "dare" comments, one that trumped all other challenges was, "I double dog dare you!" That was like "good morning, good afternoon, good night!" All challengers and challenges were exhausted.

You are "double dog dared" to keep reading this important call to a nation in free fall. There's still time to adjust our course; still time to correct our mistakes; still time to overcome our failures as a nation. But it is feared that time is not on our side. Paul issued an alarm to the Ephesian Christians (5:14-17):

"Awake, O sleeper,
and arise from the dead,
and Christ will shine on you."
Look carefully then how you walk, not as unwise but as wise, making the best use of the time, because the days are evil. Therefore do not be foolish, but understand what the will of the Lord is.

This early Christian hymn fragment called followers of Christ to awake out of slumber. So too, we are to wake up, act wisely, making the best use of our time to enact the will of God in our time. The alarm is sounding. Tones are dropping. We have no time to waste.

Please join fellow believing patriots in responding to a call for change. May a mighty movement of clear voices spread across our nation that *honor Christ the Lord as holy, always being prepared to make a defense to anyone who asks you a reason of hope that is in you, yet do it with gentleness and respect* (1 Peter 3:15). Change begins with you and me and it will affect our children, grandchildren, and generations to come.

Put on the armor of God and join the fray. The struggle will be worth it.

Looking for an Action Plan?

Search for policies and solutions to the crucial issues facing America today. As you narrow your focus of concern, you might want to consult the America First Policy Institute. You will find policy statements and information that will help you formulate an action plan for your areas of interest and concern.

The America First Policy Institute

AFPI is pursuing a robust policy agenda that puts America first and its people first. These policies are broken down into ten thematic pillars subdivided into specific policy centers, which drive towards the mission of putting the American people first.

Look at their web site to find detailed information on policies that affect your lives and our nation.

https://americafirstpolicy.com

Introduction

History has noted both men and women who take a stand for some worthy cause. They are called, "sentinels" which Webster defines simply as, "one who guards." They stand up during rain or shine. We find them faithfully standing at an assigned post regardless.

Sentinels are everywhere in our modern culture. Noteworthy are those soldiers who carry on a grand tradition at the Tomb of the Unknown Soldier. Since 1930, the Old Guard ceremonially patrols around the tomb, guarding it from desecration as well as providing information to visitors on their days off guard.

It is difficult becoming a member of this elite group. Training for this honor is rigorous indeed. Fewer than one out of ten are chosen from the ranks of the Army's 3rd Infantry Regiment to serve an 18-month tour of duty located in Washington D.C. Additional requirements include:

- Men are to be between 5 feet-10 inches and 6 feet-4 inches tall; women are to be a minimum of 5 feet-8 inches in height.

- These sentinels receive training for approximately eight months, learning the strict Tomb of the Unknown Soldier rules.

- A perfected routine walk performed at the tomb is practiced with precision.

The Tomb Guard marches exactly 21 steps down a black mat behind the Tomb, turns, facing east for 21 seconds, turns facing north for another 21 seconds and then takes 21 steps down the mat. This process repeats for every member of the Tomb Guard, 24 hours a day, seven days a week. This 21-step regiment is an illustration of a 21-

gun salute which is the highest military honor that can be bestowed. Seeing these men and women in action is among the highlights of any tour of our nation's capital.

As patriotic sentinels who influenced the Revolutionary War, Paul Revere along with William Dawes are best known for taking a "midnight ride" throughout Boston to warn Colonials of impending danger of attack from British forces. Their diligence had a direct impact on the outcome of the Battle of Lexington and Concord. Revere's refrain, "The British are coming," is classic Americana.

Then there is the diligence of Old Testament prophets who had uncommon names such as Amos, Isaiah, Zachariah, Jonah, and an eccentric firebrand known as Ezekiel. His commission was to be a watchman, a sentinel, warning people of invading forces. His admonition is preserved in a book bearing his name.

The word of the LORD came to me: "Son of man, speak to your people and say to them, If I bring the sword upon a land, and the people of the land take a man from among them, and make him their watchman, and if he sees the sword coming upon the land and blows the trumpet and warns the people, then if anyone who hears the sound of the trumpet does not take warning, and the sword comes and takes him away, his blood shall be upon his own head. He heard the sound of the trumpet and did not take warning; his blood shall be upon himself. But if he had taken warning, he would have saved his life. But if the watchman sees the sword coming and does not blow the trumpet, so that the people are not warned, and the sword comes and takes any one of them, that person is taken away in his iniquity, but his blood I will require at the watchman's hand.

—Ezekiel 33:1 - 6

Like a stone skipped across a body of water that touches the water's surface only briefly, a sentinel's touch is often only for a brief moment in time. Although the impact on their generation might be brief, powerful change results from their courage and commitment.

Yes, dedicated men and women serve at the Tomb of the Unknown Soldier. It's wondered if America might have even come into existence as a nation without fearless men like Paul Revere. Furthermore, the timeless heralds of ancient prophets serve as a continual reminder of the importance of giving warning.

Another sentinel, a forgotten guard, was responsible for saving countless lives in their day. No, they were not soldiers nor agile horsemen. They never uttered a word throughout their lives. It was a tiny bird. So small, this species could be cuddled in normal hands—of coalminers.

It was during the 19th century that canaries, known as "children of the air," became the first "risk management officer" of the coal mining industries of England and then America. Why this little bird?

Coal mining developed into a vital industry from 1850 – 1900. Demand for this black gold was growing faster than technology of the day could support. The deeper coal miners traversed into those mines, the greater risk of exposure to deadly gases that were odorless and colorless. Also, these undetectable fumes were lighter than air and highly flammable.

Canaries became a primary indicator of danger in coal mines. Carried into the shaft by a miner, these feathered warning systems could detect deadly gases by showing signs of distress when carbon monoxide was present. Canaries would die well before a human could feel the effects of any toxic gases, thus giving those miners a window of opportunity to escape the clutches of death. Canaries became popular in missions of mercy by aiding rescue operations in the aftermath of mining accidents. Coal miners found comfort in the presence of these birds. According to *Daily Mail Historical Archive*, one miner stated,

"There is something about hearing them singing when you start work that lifts the spirits. There's no doubt that collieries will be less colorful and quieter places without them."

Later, these birds became highly valued assets on the battlefields of France during the First World War. Even in the Gulf War, where deadly gases were feared to be used, a canary was "code-named ELVIS—Early Liquid Vapor Indicator System."

Today, the "canary in a coal mine" has become emblematic of risks and failures in political, economic, and cultural arenas. This imagery well describes how politics fail, economies collapse, and cultures fall into unlivable chaos.

Fellow patriots, our culture is being overwhelmed by forces of darkness, led by evil men and women who desire to change our nation into something foreign to the values and convictions foundational in the Constitution and the Bill of Rights, which are based on the authority of the Bible. Proverbial "canaries" are twitching at most every turn in our society.

Like these little birds, the call today is for you and me bravely to stand up against the tsunami of wickedness infiltrating our culture. Without an urgency to warn of impending danger, our nation might be doomed as were the passengers on the *Titanic*. How might we affect our culture? What steps are necessary to turn our nation back to her moral roots?

It means facing a swelling tide of public opposition birthed from the womb of incompetent thinking, laziness, and indifference to our culture in free-fall and the fierce, unrelenting attacks from the supernatural world of darkness.

The choice is simple. Either we hold to a biblical world view or a non-biblical world view. *A Canary in a Coal Mine: Hope for a Culture in Free Fall* is written to encourage believers in the Lord Jesus Christ to understand and return to a biblical world view. Like the sons of Issachar who *had an understanding of the times, to know what Israel ought to do* (1 Chron. 12:32), there are countless millions of patriotic Christians woven into the daily fabric of our culture who sense the need for change in our nation. Like the sons of Issachar, they understand that something is terribly wrong. And in their hearts and souls they know what needs to be done. But knowing and doing are two different things.

The call is clear. Change must come soon. Like a canary, it's time for us to become sentinels of grace and hope to a dying culture. It includes taking a firm stand against forces of darkness and those people who are controlled by them.

Midst all the chatter of noisy unbelief, it's time for our voices to be heard.

All the armies of Europe, Asia and Africa combined, with all the treasure of the earth (our own excepted) in their military chest; with a Buonaparte for a commander, could not by force, take a drink from the Ohio, or make a track on the Blue Ridge, in a Trial of a thousand years.

At what point then is the approach of danger to be expected?

I answer, if it ever reach us, it must spring up amongst us. It cannot come from abroad. If destruction be our lot, we must ourselves be its author and finisher. As a nation of freemen, we must live through all time, or die by suicide.

Abraham Lincoln

the 1838 "Lyceum Address"

Chapter One
Looking Back, Facing Forward

Everyone wants a guarantee. Guarantees touch everyday items in our lives. When purchasing a new car or having an existing model repaired, we ask about warranties. Insurance policies are secured to protect our families and investments from unexpected calamity. Benjamin Franklin, believed to have said, "the only things certain in life are death and taxes," was almost correct.

The truth is the only things certain in life are death, taxes, and supernatural discipline. Think only about the destruction of the antediluvian world: *The Lord saw that the wickedness of man was great in the earth, and that every intention of the thoughts of his heart was only evil continually. And the Lord regretted that he had made man on the earth, and it grieved him to his heart. So the Lord said, "I will blot out man whom I have created from the face of the land, man and animals and creeping things and birds of the heavens, for I am sorry that I have made them (Genesis 6:5-7)."*

Or, consider the fate of Sodom and Gomorrah. Lot, the nephew of Abraham chose to live in broad, well-watered plains of the Jordan River Valley. The occupants of the cities were wickedly depraved. God pronounced judgement upon the occupants of the cities of Sodom and Gomorrah, the cities of the Plain—*Then the Lord rained on Sodom and Gomorrah sulfur and fire from the Lord out of heaven. And he overthrew those cities, and all the valley, and all the inhabitants of the cities, and what grew on the ground (Genesis 19: 24-25).*

We are familiar with these specific instances of God's judg-

29

ment. They are world famous. They represent the breadth and depth of God's judgment against sin. One of the better known instances of God's judgement was the Flood of Genesis 7. Every culture on earth has a variation of the story. From the Epic of Gilgamesh to the Aboriginal flood accounts, they range world-wide. At least 500 legends span the globe. Many show similarities with the Genesis account. However, the morality of the Genesis account is often lacking in the other flood stories.

Note the reason for God's destruction:

- *the wickedness of man was great*
- *every intention of the thoughts of his heart was only evil continually*
- *the Lord regretted that he had made man*
- *I will blot out man whom I have created*
- *I am sorry that I have made them* (Genesis 6:5-7).

Because every intention of their heart was evil, God determined to destroy His creation. Yet, grace was extended—*But Noah found favor in the eyes of the Lord* (Gen. 6:8). God was seeding the future by extending grace to Noah. He is still seeding the future. He keeps looking for those who will stand for the right in every generation. Even Lot and his family were warned and delivered (Gen. 19:1-29).

But to be true to His nature, His attributes, justice is demanded. We might prefer the softness of mercy. But mercy without justice isn't just. Mercy without justice is license. It is no true compassion. It is merely indulgence. Attendant to the mercy of God is His justice. And justice demands judgment upon unrighteousness and evil.

God has not changed His mind about His determined goal for humanity. However, humanity often gets in the way of God and the end is their own destruction. We do well to recall the word of the Lord: *For the eyes of the Lord run to and fro throughout the whole earth, to give strong support to those whose heart is blameless toward him* (2 Chron. 16:9a). But do not forget that while God will give strong support to those who seek His way, He will not be mocked: *Do not be deceived: God is not mocked, for whatever one sows, that will he also reap* (Galatians 6:7). Many have sown seeds of corruption and are praying for a crop failure.

Do not mistake the forbearance of God as permission. The Apostle John stated that God's *judgments are true and just* (Rev. 19:2). And although the judgments of God might be tempered and delayed by His mercy, they will come upon those who turn away from Him and His ways. God considers the whole scope of a nation (Ezekiel 16:48-50). Any delay is an opportunity to repent and turn from wickedness: *Do you presume on the riches of his kindness and forbearance and patience, not knowing that God's kindness is meant to lead you to repentance? But because of your hard and impenitent heart you are storing up wrath for yourself on the day of wrath when God's righteous judgment will be revealed* (Romans 2:4-5).

Death and taxes? Guaranteed. God's judgment? Guaranteed!

That goes for nations past and present—including America. An informed biblical world view grasps the somber truth that nations come and go. Peoples and cultures who existed thousands of years ago are now on the ash heap of history. And though our nation is alive today, we have no guarantee about tomorrow. Our end will be determined by our willingness to seek the way of the Lord.

Two Kinds of History

Remember, two kinds of history are occurring. One is human history. It is marked at Creation and continues to this day. But paralleling human history is the biblical record of Genesis through Revelation—redemptive history. Both continue simultaneously.

People often want to treat the Bible as a history book. And it is of sorts. It is the record of God's intended will to create for Himself a people. The Bible is the story of God's redemption of His creation and the fulfillment of His desire to create for Himself a people. Some say, "The Bible is HIS-story." (Note the following chart.)

31

World Empires	All dates B.C.	Biblical History
2334 2154 { The Akkadian Empire: the first world empire { The Dynasty of Ur exerted power after the fall of the Akkadian Empire	2267- 1992 {	Abram of Ur called by God to leave and go to a land He would show him
2025 The Assyrian Empire While its power and dominance waxed and waned over the centuries, the Assyrian Empire was the dominant world power for over 1400 years.	1500	Moses
	1000	King David
	760	The Ministry of Amos begins
	739	The Ministries of Micah and Isaiah begin
	722	Israel: Northern Kingdom falls to the Assyrians— dispersed and disappears
612 The Babylonian Empire	605	Judah: Southern Kingdom taken captive to Babylon
536 Persian overthrow of the Babylonian Empire.	536	Release of Jews from Babylon captivity by Persian King Cyrus
	400	The Old Testament revelation ends
332 Persian Empire falls to Alexander the Great		
142 Jewish Independence ends Greek domination		
63 Rome occupies Palestine		

To accomplish His purpose, God called a man from Mesopotamia, Abram of Ur, to be the founder of a lineage that would be instrumental in achieving His purpose. Abram was from the Mesopotamian Valley, the Fertile Crescent.

This area was the birthplace of empires. The first great empire, the Akkadian Empire, came from this very area. The city of Accad is mentioned in Genesis 10:10. It was from this name that the Akkadian Empire took its name. It rose around 2334 B.C. from an invading people group who came into the region and began the acquisition of resources (the usual reason empires develop). It fell in 2154 B.C. because of exhausted resources brought on by changing climate and the attendant natural phenomena.

For instance, recent discoveries have found that deep layers of dust blew into the rich farming land of the Mesopotamian Valley. An extended drought starved the crops for water and, in turn, the parched land starved the Akkadian Empire. As the dust storms, like those of the Dust Bowl of the American mid-west, covered the rich, but parched land of the Mesopotamian Valley, the Akkadian Empire was relegated to the dust bin of history. But it would be followed in a very brief time by the Assyrian Empire.

The Assyrian Empire began around 2000 B.C. and would last as a major power in the Mesopotamian region until 612 B.C. (Some have dated the earliest beginnings around 2500 B.C. with various iterations waxing and waning in power and prominence.) As early as Genesis 10:11, Assyria is mentioned. Even with a 1400-year imperial reign, the Assyrians would fall. More on this later.

It is worth noting that the empires of the world order are of little import to the biblical account. Since the Bible is an account of redemptive history, the empires and nations of the world are only of importance as they relate directly to the redemption story.

The careful study of history reveals that present day nations are on the same path to extinction as past empires. The rise and fall of empires date back thousands of years to the earliest form of empire.

The reasons for the rise and fall of empires are not mysteries.

The Collapse of Empires

Empires fall for a variety of reasons. Consider these causes:

1. *They are conquered by an external enemy.* Examples: The Eastern Roman Empire, the Babylonian Empire, the Achaemenid Persian Empire, the Incan Empire, the Aztec Empire.

2. *They debase their currency, destroy their economy, and go bankrupt.* Examples: The Western Roman Empire (a contributor to the Crisis of the Third Century), the Spanish Empire, the British Empire.

3. *They do not manage to sort out succession of power.* Examples: The Mongol Empire, the Macedon Empire of Alexander, the Hunnic Empire, the Western Roman Empire, the Ottoman Empire.

4. *They rule incompetently and break from inside.* Examples: The Russian Empire, the Assyrian Empire.

5. *They create or fall prey to an ecological catastrophe.* Examples: The Akkadian Empire—an extended drought and dust storms helped end the Akkadian Empire; the Maya Empire—exhausted the resources of its empire and fell from great heights.

6. *They lose belief in themselves; their confidence and empirical image is diminished.* Example: the Soviet Union (to an extent).

7. *They decay morally/ethically from within.* In this weakened condition, the will and competency to resist external threats are destroyed. Thus, they collapse with little effort by outside forces. Examples: The Hellenistic Empire, the Roman Empire.

8. *They over-extend their resources.* Usually collapse is inaugurated by the placement of military installations in the hinterlands of the territories the empire attempts to control. Examples: Roman Empire, the British Empire, the Napoleonic Empire, the Macedon Empire of Alexander, the Hunnic Empire of Attila.

All of these factors are not required to bring down an empire. It can be a combination of some or all that cause an empire to decline or extinguish itself. If an empire can avoid all of them, it might endure indefinitely. But that has never proven to be the case.

The Birth of a Nation

Empires give birth to nations. Less than 500 years has passed since Spain, France, and Britain were in heated competition to discover new lands for their respective empires. Massive territories stretching around the world came under their rule. For instance, the British Empire at its height controlled a quarter of all land on earth.

The territories and colonies of the North and South American Continents were born out of such imperialism. In North America, it took several decades for thirteen colonies to form what would become the United States of America. The soil of this young nation would be stained with the blood of brave men and women who sought to be free from the tyrannies of European control.

A high price for freedom would be exacted from the Colonies. Though preceded by years of unrest and periodic conflict, the Revolutionary War began in earnest on April 19, 1775 with battles fought at Lexington and Concord. On July 4, 1776, America was born with the Declaration of Independence.

Fifty-six brave men who signed the Declaration understood the dangers of declaring independence from an earthly power. The last line of the Declaration of Independence ends with a pledge the signers made to one another—"We Mutually Pledge To Each Other Our Lives, Our Fortunes, And Our Sacred Honor…"

Patriots call to patriots over the centuries.

SoldierStrong has stated: "With this last sentence of our Declaration of Independence, the fifty-six signers of that document not only committed themselves to uncompromising, complete devotion to the American Republic, but they also charted a path for all patriots to come. When the signers of the Declaration committed themselves to this pledge, they also signed the warrants for their own doom at the hands of the greatest military force the world had known to that point. It's not that they did not know whether Washington and the Continental Army would be successful. Quite to the contrary, there was little reason to believe they would. This is what makes their commitment so very courageous." (https://www.soldierstrong.org, July 25, 2017—*SoldierStrong* is the national veteran-focused nonprofit resourcing and supporting veterans.)

Steve Chabot has written of the danger posed to the signatories. His observations are based on Benjamin Franklin's remark, "We must all hang together, or most assuredly, we will all hang separately." Chabot writes:

"Benjamin Franklin made this statement at the signing of the Declaration of Independence in 1776. He was of course referring to the need for the signers and the states they represented, to stick together against a common enemy, Great Britain. He knew the only chance the colonies had in facing the most powerful army and nation on the face of the earth, was to remain united in their resolve to achieve independence. Although Franklin's words were said 240 years ago, they should ring just as true to every right-thinking citizen in America today." (from: https://stevechabot.com/blog/we-must-all-hang-together-or-most-assuredly-we-will-all-hang-separately/ May 11, 2016)

As wonderful, sobering, and challenging as these words of commitment to one another were, it is the preceding words that state their dependence upon Almighty God. It was not just by their actions and their commitment to one another that this nation was established. But it was from their dependence upon Almighty God that this nation was established.

The fuller statement of those closing words of this document stated: "For the support of this declaration, **with a firm reliance on the protection of Divine Providence**, we mutually pledge to each other our lives, our fortunes and our sacred honor."

Seven years later, the Revolutionary War ended when British forces were removed from Charleston, South Carolina and Savannah, Georgia in 1782. America was on the road to becoming a great nation. The single reason of her greatness is because the Lord's gracious hand of blessing rests upon us.

- Our greatness is because of the vast landscape stretching from the Atlantic to the Pacific Oceans. Rich resources including timber, water, ore, and oil have blessed us for centuries.

- Our greatness is found in the citizenry. The pioneer spirit continues to be a hallmark quality of our culture. Daniel Boone, Lewis and Clark, Neil Armstrong highlight such drive.

- Our greatness is due to our system of government. America is NOT a democracy. It was established as a Republic. What's the difference? A democracy is "majority rule of people," whereas a Republic is a representative government. Why is that important? A Republic provides equality for states in less populated areas. That means Montana has two senators just like California. Congress also has the House of Representatives. Every representative seat is determined by population.

- Our greatness is found in our generous spirit. America is a leader in assisting other nations who struggle with poverty, weather calamities, or oppression.

- Our greatness is due to the freedom we enjoy. Ten freedoms are outlined and enshrined in the Bill of Rights that include speech, press, religion, assembly, and bearing arms.

- Our freedoms are anchored to the Bible. Samuel Rutherford, a Presbyterian minister challenged the 17th century principle of the divine rights of a king. He asserted that the Bible alone stands as basis of authority. God's Word, not the word of any man, would be that authority. This mindset was at the heart of writing the Constitution. A Judeo-Christian ethic remains at the heart of the laws of our land.

Our founders' convictions about God's Word influenced higher education across the nation. Almost every "Ivy League" school including Harvard, established in 1638; Yale, 1701; Princeton, 1746; and Dartmouth, 1754 were established primarily to train ministers of the gospel who would evangelize the Atlantic seaboard.

Our nation's symbols boast of faith in the Lord. The Supreme Court has a crier who opens each session with the traditional interjection that includes the phrase: "God save the United States and the Honorable Court." Moses and the Ten Commandments are depicted on the South Frieze of the courtroom in the Supreme Court Building.

Those who constructed the Washington Monument lined the inner walls with Scriptures, *"Holiness to the Lord,"* *"Search the Scriptures,"* and *"Train up a child in the way he should go, and when he is old he will not depart from it."* No building in Washington is permitted to be taller than the Washington Monument. The great monument is capped with an inscribed aluminum cap. Notable names and dates in the monument's construction are recalled. But on the east side facing the rising sun, the Latin words, *Laus Deo*, are inscribed. These words translate to, "Praise be to God." Over the capital of our nation, the designers and builders fixed words that they wanted to represent God looking over this nation.

The wall of the Lincoln Memorial has etched on it the entire body of the Gettysburg Address, a stirring speech that reminds us, *"the judgments of the Lord are true and righteous altogether."* Every form of our nation's currency testifies, "In God we trust."

Like rudders to a ship, God raised up sentinels to guide this nation through good times and hard times. Jonathan Edwards, George

Whitefield, and other firebrands were instrumental in ushering in spiritual movements called the First Great Awakening and the Second Great Awakening. This spiritual influence buoyed our culture as she protected a tender heart toward things of the Lord.

Sadly, after all the blessings having been bestowed upon our culture, a noticeable move away from the things of the Lord is operational across our nation at an accelerated pace. When this free-fall began is debatable. Some believe it started when prayer (and later copies of the Ten Commandments) was removed from public schools; others point to corruption in our federal government; still others think a distinction between the affluent and the welfare state is the culprit. One fact remains. A struggle for the soul of our culture is raging.

It is an undisputed truth that America and her people have been a "shining light on the hill" for centuries. Our allies have been strengthened. Adversaries weakened or removed. Multiple wars and conflicts have dotted the landscape of our nation's history. We have been a superpower since dropping atomic weapons on two Japanese cities to hasten the end of World War II. Our military strength is often the envy of the world. And as long as the conflicts were done on the side of goodness, not greed and godlessness, our nation too remained the envy of the world.

However, where once we were a mighty global military and economic force, today our nation is reeling from decay within caused by another kind of conflict—a cultural conflict.

How is that possible and what might that look like?

We will explore some of the primary threats to the nation in these pages. The "Culture Killers." The issues that can lead to the demise of a temporal kingdom. While we will not address every aspect of the perceived threats, you will have enough to inform and to engage you in saving our nation.

Steps to take now:

Action # 1: Read the Declaration of Independence.

Action # 2: Get a copy of the Constitution and Bill of Rights and read them.

Action # 3: Register to vote to secure your fundamental rights and vote in every election available to you.

Action # 4: Meditate on Nehemiah chapter one using a favorite Bible translation.

Chapter Two
Dual Citizenship

Recall Daniel in the lions' den. A wonderful story we learn as children. The images of the teaching pictures we saw in Bible school still flash across our memories at just the mention of the story.

But it is not just an interesting Bible story. It is the clash of kingdoms. The Kingdom of God and the kingdoms of this world.

Christians have tended to stress their citizenship in the Kingdom of God more than their citizenship in whatever temporal kingdom they live. Sometimes it is to the detriment of their effectiveness and witness in this world. The phrase—"So heavenly-minded that they are of no earthly good"—comes to mind. The concept took tangible expression in some significant ways throughout history.

Monasticism and other withdrawal strategies were adopted by the Christian community. These separation strategies separated those in the Kingdom of God from the temporal kingdoms in which they lived.

• *The Desert Fathers (and Mothers) practiced asceticism.* The first of these men was Anthony of Egypt. He went into the desert of Egypt to live as a hermit. He went to live for God, just to be able to spend his life fasting and praying, fighting with the demons.

Others followed his example. They were radically sold-out people. They turned their backs on temporal kingdoms and focused exclusively on the Kingdom of God.

• *In the Monastic Movement, Christians cloistered away from the world.* The withdrawal from society that began with the Desert Fathers morphed into the early expression of the monastic movement. One wit quipped that cenobitic (community focused) monasticism is "a collection of loners." Gradually, this life of separation became an influential model for the larger Christian community.

While everyone might not be able to retreat into the monasteries, the monastic life became an influence on the way Christians would engage the world—or not.

A spiritualizing direction began to see being tied to this world with the values of family, employment, and engagement as bad. Following the models of the Desert Fathers and the Monastic Movement, Christians adopted separation from the world as a mindset ever since—whether you are in a monastery or not.

This separation from the world evidenced itself in some Christian sects pulling away to live in isolated communities such as the Shakers of the 18th century or the Amish. They wished to maintain holiness by limiting contact with and the influence of the world.

These expressions are ways to live the Christian life. However, they might not match the more complete teaching of Scripture. This is not to impugn the sincerity or the devotion of these groups. These are valid personal and community expressions of faith. The behavior of believers should reflect the holiness of God. But in addition to that holiness is the responsibility of Christian citizenship.

How are we to live in relation to the world systems?

Daniel, the prophet, helps us understand how we navigate the demands on us as the people of God of both the spiritual kingdom and the temporal kingdoms in which we live.

Orchestrating Nations

As we consider how we are to interact with world systems, bear in mind this truth: God establishes kingdoms and sets their parameters.

In His transcendence and omniscience, He causes empires and nations to rise and fall. Read these passages of Scripture to set the direction for our thinking about how we, as Christians, are to interface with our culture and the temporal kingdoms of this world.

Psalms 22:28—*For kingship belongs to the Lord, and he rules over the nations.*

Job 12:23—*He makes the nations great, then destroys them; He enlarges the nations, then leads them away.*

Acts 17:26—*and He made from one man every nation of mankind to live on all the face of the earth, having determined their appointed times and the boundaries of their habitation,*

Daniel 2:21—*He changes times and seasons; he removes kings and sets up kings; he gives wisdom to the wise and knowledge to those who have understanding;*

The testimony of history and of Scripture affirms that God moves kings and kingdoms to achieve His purposes. For instance:

God used the Assyrians to remove the Northern Tribes for their relentless disobedience. The Northern Tribes were utterly destroyed as a people. The Assyrians dispersed and absorbed them so thoroughly that they are referred to as the Ten Lost Tribes of Israel (2 Kings 18:11-12).

But the Assyrians had to be removed in order for the plan of God for redemption to be fulfilled (Is. 14:24-25). The Assyrian policy toward captives of dispersion and absorption could not be allowed to play out with the Southern Tribes. God had to retain a remnant in order for His plan of redemption to be fulfilled.

So God raised up the Babylonians in order for them to discipline the Southern Kingdom. Their policy toward captives was to keep them intact as a people group. They were used as labor, with the upper classes used in the court of the king. Any of the young men selected to serve in the king's court had to be put through a re-education program to teach the languages and other necessary skills. It is in this situation that we are first introduced to Daniel and his three cohorts that we know as Shadrach, Meshach, and Abednego.

The Babylonian Empire did not last long. Just long enough to serve God's purpose of disciplining the Southern Tribes through exile. Actually, the Babylonian Empire we encounter in the Bible is the Neo-Babylonian Empire, which lasted from 626 B.C. to 539 B.C. It became the most powerful state in the world after defeating the Assyrians at Nineveh in 612 B.C. Within three years, it dominated the world. But in 539 B.C., less than a century after its founding, it was swept into the dust bin of history. It had fulfilled its purpose.

God raised up the Medo-Persian Empire to continue His plan of redemption through the Jewish nation. Cyrus, king of the Persians, was named by the prophet Isaiah as the *Anointed One of God.* He was chosen to release the Jews from captivity, ending their exile. He even provided the means and resources for rebuilding the Temple in Jerusalem. God called him by name 176 years before Cyrus actually released the Jews from captivity. (See Is. 44:28; 45:1-7.)

who says of Cyrus, 'He is my shepherd,
and he shall fulfill all my purpose';
saying of Jerusalem, 'She shall be built,'
and of the temple, 'Your foundation shall be laid (44:28).'"

Remember, God orchestrates the rise and fall of nations to achieve His purposes.

The Hand of God in Human Events

Dr. J. Vernon McGee has spoken eloquently of Providence:

"What is providence? Here's a theological definition: Providence is the means by which God directs all things—both animate and inanimate, seen and unseen, good and evil—toward a worthy purpose, which means His will must finally prevail. Or as the psalmist said, *"his kingdom ruleth over all"* (Psalm 103:19 KJV). In Ephesians 1:11 Paul tells us that God *"worketh all things after the counsel of his own will* (KJV)." Our God is running the universe today, friends, even though there are some who think that it has slipped out from under Him.

"Providence means that the hand of God is in the glove of human events. When God is not at the steering wheel, He is the backseat driver. He is the coach who calls the signals from the bench. Providence is the unseen rudder on the ship of state. God is the pilot at the wheel during the night watch. As someone has said, *"He makes great doors swing on little hinges."* God brought together a little baby's cry and a woman's heart down by the River Nile when Pharaoh's daughter went to bathe. The Lord pinched little Moses and he let out a yell. The cry reached the heart of the princess, and God used it to change the destiny of a people. That was providence. That was the hand of God." (*Edited Messages on Esther*)

We look around our nation today and we ask, "Is God in control?" We will do well to remember that God's hand is still and always will be in the glove of our human events.

Opening the Lock of History

Daniel was given the key that opens the lock of history. It came through a disturbing dream that King Nebuchadnezzar had. The four Hebrew teenagers (Daniel, Shadrach, Meshach, and Abednego), now living in exile in Babylon, had just completed their training. They were to serve in the court of the king.

The king had a frightful dream. A nightmare. He would not reveal it to any of his court. But he demanded that his wise men tell him what the dream was and what was its meaning. They were all stymied. The king threatened to kill them all and that included Daniel and his friends.

With the king refusing to divulge the dream, the wise men could not tell the dream nor the interpretation. The king flew into a violent rage and commanded his chief executioner, Arioch, to kill them all. Including Daniel. Daniel had already distinguished himself in their training. Arioch explained the situation to the young Hebrew. With nothing to lose but his life, Daniel approached the king asking for time so he could discern the dream and its meaning.

Daniel went to his home and asked his friends to pray seeking mercy from God that he would receive the dream and interpretation. In the night, the revelation was given. Daniel's prayer is instructive:

> *"Blessed be the name of God forever and ever,*
> *to whom belong wisdom and might.*
> *He changes times and seasons;*
> **he removes kings and sets up kings;**
> *he gives wisdom to the wise*
> *and knowledge to those who have understanding;*
> *he reveals deep and hidden things;*
> *he knows what is in the darkness,*
> *and the light dwells with him.*
> *To you, O God of my fathers,*
> *I give thanks and praise,*
> *for you have given me wisdom and might,*
> *and have now made known to me what we asked of you,*
> *for you have made known to us the king's matter."*

Here's what God revealed: The king had seen a huge and terrifying statue of a man. The statue was made of mixed metals. The head was gold, the chest and arms were of silver, the stomach and thighs were of bronze, the legs and feet were of iron with the feet a mixture of iron and clay. The final part of the dream was of a stone that crushed the statue and all the various metals.

The meaning of the dream revealed hundreds of years of the future. The various metals in the statue represented four kingdoms (present and future) that would control the Jews and their lands.

• The gold represented the Babylonian kingdom—612-539 B.C.

- The silver represented the Medo-Persians—539-331 B.C.
- The bronze represented the Greeks—331-146 B.C.
- The iron and clay represented the Roman Empire—63 B.C.-A.D. 1453.

The stone that crushed the statue and the other metals was the Kingdom of God that would be established forever, ruling over all kingdoms and people of the earth.

The Kingdom of the Stone

The Old Testament has numerous prophetic references to the Stone:

- Psalm 118:22—the Stone rejected by the builders becomes the chief cornerstone
- Isaiah 14:14-15—the Stumbling Stone
- Isaiah 28:16—The Foundation Stone
- Daniel 2:34-35; 44-45—The Kingdom of the Stone, not cut by human hands, would fill the entire earth

Throughout the New Testament, at key instances and in primary theological teachings, the Stone is referred to from these Old Testament passages. Time and space does not allow exploration of these texts. However, you might want to do that study on your own. See—

- Matthew 16:16,18
- Matthew 21:42
- Acts 4:11
- Romans 9:33
- 1 Corinthians 3:10-17
- Ephesians 2:20-22
- 1 Peter 2:4-10

The Stone represented a kingdom that God was establishing that would crush the other kingdoms and fill the world. It would be a kingdom that came into being in a unique manner through the life, death, and resurrection of Jesus.

Jesus connected His ministry with the Kingdom of God after He had healed a demoniac who was blind and mute. The healing was so dramatic that the crowds began asking if Jesus could be the promised Messiah. Members of the legalistic and powerful sect, the Pharisees, heard those comments and accused Jesus of being possessed Himself.

Jesus responded by saying that a kingdom divided against itself cannot stand. Abraham Lincoln quoted this during his run for the Senate. It famously became known as his "House Divided" speech. Lincoln opened with these words:

"A house divided against itself, cannot stand."

I believe this government cannot endure permanently half slave and half free.

I do not expect the Union to be dissolved – I do not expect the house to fall – but I do expect it will cease to be divided.

It will become all one thing or all the other.

We would be wise to remember these words in the current condition of our nation. It seems that we might be as divided at this moment as we have been since the Civil War. We are being fractured in a thousand ways. The nation is under attack from the center to the circumference and at all 360° points of the circumference. We cannot long endure this division and these attacks.

Jesus connected His Spirit-empowered ministry to the Kingdom of God: *But if it is by the Spirit of God that I cast out demons, then the kingdom of God has come upon you* (Matt. 12:28).

As He stood before Pontius Pilate on trial before His crucifixion, Jesus was asked if He was a king.

Jesus answered, "My kingdom is not of this world. If my kingdom were of this world, my servants would have been fighting, that I might not be delivered over to the Jews. But my kingdom is not from the world."

In this exchange, Jesus noted the existence of two kingdoms. The kingdom He was establishing and the kingdoms of this world.

He had done this earlier in a different way. On Tuesday during the week of Passover, the enemies of Jesus, the Pharisees and the Herodians, tried to trap Him with a question about taxes. Now, listen up—this is important!

Jesus responded to them: *Bring me a denarius and let me look at it." And they brought one. And he said to them, "Whose likeness and inscription is this?" They said to him, "Caesar's." Jesus said to them, "Render to Caesar the things that are Caesar's, and to God the things that are God's." And they marveled at him.*

In His response, Jesus drew a distinction between the things that are Caesar's and the things that are God's. Two kingdoms: a temporal kingdom and the Kingdom of God. What is the Christian's responsibility? How do we relate to these two domains?

The answer to these questions are core to our understanding of what we are to be doing in this present age and particularly in our nation.

Jesus and the Kingdom of God

The Kingdom of God was the central theme of the ministry of Jesus The phrase, *Kingdom of God,* has three primary meanings or usages in the ministry of Jesus.

<u>First, God is eternally King</u>. The Psalmist understood this—

All the ends of the world shall remember and turn unto the LORD: and all the kindreds of the nations shall worship before thee.
For the kingdom is the LORD'S: and he is the governor among the nations (Ps. 22:27-28 KJV).

Jesus expressed this same concept in the Model Prayer: *After this manner therefore pray ye: Our Father which art in heaven, Hallowed be thy name.*
Thy kingdom come. Thy will be done in earth, as it is in heaven.
Give us this day our daily bread.
And forgive us our debts, as we forgive our debtors.
And lead us not into temptation, but deliver us from evil: For thine is

the kingdom, and the power, and the glory, for ever. Amen (Matt. 6:9-13 KJV).

By virtue of His creation, God is eternally King.

<u>Second, God will establish an end-time Kingdom</u> when the reign of God will be established throughout the world. In His eschatological teachings in Matthew 24-25, Jesus spoke of this end-time kingdom: *'Come, you who are blessed by my Father, inherit the kingdom prepared for you from the foundation of the world* (Matt. 25:34).

At the Last Supper, Jesus referred to this end-time kingdom. As He instituted what we refer to as the Lord's Supper, He stated: *Truly, I say to you, I will not drink again of the fruit of the vine until that day when I drink it new in the kingdom of God* (Mark 14:25)."

<u>Third, the rule and reign of God in the heart and life of an individual</u>. The vast majority of the time Jesus spoke of the kingdom of God (about 90%), He addressed the rule of God in an individual's life. One of the better moments that helps us understand this internal dimension of the Kingdom of God in a person's life is found in an exchange between Jesus and a scribe detailed in Mark 12: 28-34. Note what Jesus said to the man—*And when Jesus saw that he answered wisely, he said to him, "You are not far from the kingdom of God." And after that no one dared to ask him any more questions.*

When Jesus said that he was not far from the kingdom of God, He was not telling the scribe that he was going to die or that the end-time kingdom was about to be inaugurated. He was stating that this man was not far from God ruling and reigning upon the throne of his life.

This dimension of the kingdom of God is about lordship. Who rules in our lives? Who sits upon the throne of our hearts? Us? Or God? Are we egocentric? Or theocentric. Self-centered? Or God-centered?

The difference between us and Jesus is that every person who has ever existed at some time, committed the same rebellion that Adam committed. We chose our way over God's way. Our choice was to obey or not. We chose not to obey. That choice led to our separation from God, our spiritual deaths (James 1:13-15).

The kingdom of God is not about a territory. It is not about a physical throne. It is about people—people who seek the will of God. God is gathering from all peoples of the earth, those who allow God to rule their lives. That is the kingdom of God.

Those who faith God are part of the Kingdom of God. It is God to whom we give allegiance.

And that is where the rub comes. When the Kingdom of God conflicts with the kingdoms of men, the people of God must make a choice of where their loyalties lie.

The Central Theme

The central theme of Jesus' ministry was the *kingdom of God*. In the Gospels, the phrase, *kingdom of heaven*, appears thirty-two times, uttered by Jesus thirty times; the phrase, *kingdom of God*, appears fifty-two times, uttered by Jesus forty-four times—both phrases are interchangeable.

The statistics alone show how important this concept was to Jesus. The *kingdom of God* also appears in every aspect of the Jesus' ministry. The prayer life of Jesus inspired His disciples to request: *Lord, teach us to pray* (Luke 11:1 KJV). Matthew provides summaries of the ministry of Jesus: *And Jesus went about all the cities and villages, teaching in their synagogues, and preaching the gospel of the kingdom, and healing every sickness and every disease among the people* (see Matt. 4:23; 9:35 KJV).

Explore the following references to see how the Kingdom of God filled each of these actions in the life of Jesus:

- Praying—Matthew 6:9-13.

- Teaching—Acts 1:3.

- Preaching—Mark 1:14-15.

- Healing—Matthew 12:28.

Jesus not only taught about the kingdom of God—the will of God in a person's life—He modeled what it was to be ruled by God's will.

Total Submission

The writer of Hebrews referenced the excruciating moment of prayer in the Garden (Hebrews 5:7-10). Although Jesus could have prayed to be delivered, He submitted Himself to the will of the Father in every regard, even when facing death, the horrible death on the cross (Phil. 2:8).

Twenty-first century citizens of democracies have difficulty grasping the idea of kingdom. Submitting to the rule of a king is foreign to most. A better way to conceive the concept of kingdom is to think of the kingdom of God as the will of God in our lives.

Jesus Himself pursued the will of God at every juncture: *My food is to do the will of Him who sent Me, and to accomplish His work* (John 4:34). He exhibited the lifestyle that pleases God.

For Jesus, obeying God's will was a matter of the heart, the way to love God. Obeying the will of God cost Jesus His life. At Gethsemane, the shadow of the cross shrouded Him. Imminent death, however, did not shake His resolve nor weaken His submission to the Father. He prayed, *Not My will, but Thine be done* (Luke 22:42b).

Following that will eventually took Him into the court of Pilate, the Roman governor, and on to the Cross of Golgotha. On that cross, Jesus was the sin-bearer and the sacrifice for the sins of the whole world. By that act of atonement, Jesus established a New Covenant with all who come to Him in faith. We who accept this New Covenant are made part of the Kingdom of God.

Dual Citizenship

Regardless of nationality, we who faith God through Jesus Christ have been transferred into the kingdom of His dear Son. Paul wrote the Colossian Christians: *He has delivered us from the domain of darkness and transferred us to the kingdom of his beloved Son, in whom we have redemption, the forgiveness of sins* (Col. 1:13-14).

Through our faith, God has accepted us and given us a right standing before Him. By faith we have a new and different citizenship (Phil. 3:20). In Christ, we become citizens of another kingdom—the Kingdom of God.

The Kingdom of God is about people. It spans the whole of humanity. The superficial characteristics of race, gender, nationality, economic condition, or status in life no longer matter. Paul caught this idea when he stated—*for in Christ Jesus you are all sons of God, through faith. For as many of you as were baptized into Christ have put on Christ. There is neither Jew nor Greek, there is neither slave nor free, there is no male and female, for you are all one in Christ Jesus. And if you are Christ's, then you are Abraham's offspring, heirs according to promise* (Gal. 3:26-29).

He said the same thing to the Colossian Christians: *Here there is not Greek and Jew, circumcised and uncircumcised, barbarian, Scythian, slave, free; but Christ is all, and in all* (Col. 3:11).

From all the peoples of the earth, God has gathered a people—the *laos* of God, through faith in Jesus Christ. The great division of humanity is whether we are citizens of the Kingdom of God or not.

But we are still citizens of the various temporal kingdoms and nations in which we physically abide. The relationship of the Christian with the Kingdom of God and the temporal kingdoms is intertwined.

- God has called His people out from the fallen world system. The word for "church" is *ekklesia* meaning the called-out-ones. This is reflected in Peter's description of the people of God: *But you are a chosen race, a royal priesthood, a holy nation, a people for his own possession, that you may proclaim the excellen-*

cies of him who <u>called you out</u> of darkness into his marvelous light. Once you were not a people, but now you are God's people; once you had not received mercy, but now you have received mercy (1 Pet. 2:9-10). God has called us out of darkness into light; out of sin into righteousness; out of death into life.

- But He has not taken us out of this physical world.

- Rather, He has sent us back into the world—not to be of the world but to proclaim His grace and forgiveness in the world.

And so we have dual citizenship—in the Kingdom of God and in the kingdoms of this world. We have responsibilities in both kingdoms. However, one of these citizenships holds a greater weight of loyalty than the other.

Steps to take now:

Action # 1: Lead in establishing an Intercessory Prayer Ministry for our nation at your church.

Action # 2: Collect contact information of your United States' Representative and Senators including phone numbers and email addresses. Add the information to your phone and email contacts to make communication as easy and efficient as possible.

Action # 3: Select chapters of *A Canary in a Coal Mine* that are concerning and discuss the subjects with your circles of influence.

Chapter Three
Kingdoms in Conflict

When conflict comes between the Kingdom of God and the kingdoms of this world, we must choose to be loyal first and foremost to the Kingdom of God. The early Christians knew this experientially.

When Peter and John were brought before the Jewish authorities for preaching about Jesus, they were told to stop doing this. They responded to the Sanhedrin—*Whether it is right in the sight of God to listen to you rather than to God, you must judge, for we cannot but speak of what we have seen and heard* (Acts 4:19-20).

Peter and John defied the warning because they had greater loyalty to God than to men. This is the heart of the conflict that defines our day. If the conflict is between obeying God or obeying men—God wins. That is where our loyalty resides.

A Test of Loyalty
Remember our brother, Daniel. When our curtain rose on our last chapter, Daniel was in the lions' den. He was put there because of a conflict of kingdoms—the Kingdom of God and the kingdom of Medo-Persia.

What is sometimes missed is that Daniel was an old man when he was thrown into the lions' den. Probably 81-82. He had been taken to Babylon when he was 15. At 18, he interpreted Nebuchadnezzar's dream and was elevated to a powerful position in the service of the king. He retained a place of honor all his days.

When the Babylonian Empire fell to Cyrus and the Medo-

Persians, Daniel was given a place of honor and power in the new regime. Darius, the ruler of the Medes, especially was impressed with the wisdom and character of Daniel. In fact, Daniel was made one of three presidents to help administer the Empire. He so distinguished himself that Darius was appointing him as the chief administrator over the entire kingdom.

The other administrators realized that their power and authority was to be limited. They tried to find a charge they could bring against Daniel, but they could find none. They did, however, find a weakness—his faith in and devotion to Jehovah God.

Daniel prayed three times each day facing Jerusalem, his homeland. They persuaded the king to write an edict that no one was to pray to or petition any other god or man other than the king for 30 days. Daniel continued to pray just as he had always done. The penalty for violation—to be thrown into the lions' den, a form of capital punishment.

The law once written could not be changed—even by the king himself. (The phrase "the Law of the Medes and Persians" was inspired by this text in Daniel. It means an unalterable, immutable decree.) Dismayed, King Darius commanded Daniel thrown to the lions. He commended Daniel to his God (Dan. 6:16).

Daniel only declared his innocence AFTER he came out of the lions' den (Dan. 6:21–22). Surviving the night in the lions' den was proof of Daniel's innocence. The Greek Septuagint version of the Bible states that the "accusers" were the other two administrators, not necessarily the entire lot of 120 satraps. It makes sense that it was not all of the satraps. That level of collusion would have been difficult to bring together. But two? Yes. Too bad for them.

Turn of the Table—the Dinner Table

The king had the accusers and their families thrown into the lions' den. Daniel's accusers had not even reached the bottom before the lions had attacked and crushed all their bones. They died while

Daniel lived an honored life, long enough to see his people, freed by Cyrus, the Persian, return to Jerusalem.

The story ended badly for Daniel's accusers. The lions' dinner table was turned on them.

King Darius recognized the power of Daniel's God, Jehovah. He commanded the people of his kingdom to worship Jehovah (Dan. 6:25–27). Through Daniel's deliverance, King Darius and his kingdom came to know and reverence Jehovah, the God of Daniel. *"For he is the living God and he endures forever; his kingdom will not be destroyed, his dominion will never end."*

In the situation, Daniel had a choice to make. Maintain his faith in God or submit to the dictates of the temporal kingdom. He chose to put his faith in God. God intervened and protected Daniel. God does not always send an angel to protect us. Ask all those who died in the Roman Empire's persecutions. And all the others who have died at the hands of hostile states. But in every instance, we are called to seek the will of God above all.

The world system is against the things of God. And the world will muzzle us and make us serfs. Jesus said that we should expect hatred from the world. It hated Him and it will hate His followers: *If the world hates you, understand that it hated Me first. If you were of the world, it would love you as its own. Instead, the world hates you, because you are not of the world, but I have chosen you out of the world* (Jn. 15:18-19). To underscore this animosity, recall the persecutions under Nero, Decius, and Diocletian. These Roman emperors targeted the early Christian community.

While we might not be called upon to be imprisoned or to die for our faith, we must still determine our loyalties.

Responsibilities

Until we enter the gates of the end-time kingdom, we have responsibility to live under the authority of the governments of the nations in which we reside. Whether it be the tyranny of dictators as in the

Roman Empire. Or whether it be in the wonderful Republic of the United States.

The apostolic canaries, Paul and Peter, both instruct us on how we are to conduct ourselves in relation to the governments of the temporal kingdoms in which we live.

Paul, as a Roman/Jewish citizen, understood as much as anyone the demands of the two kingdoms upon the Christian. He recognized that we are citizens of the Kingdom of God. He states this a couple of different ways in his letters to the churches:

To the Philippian Christians:
But our citizenship is in heaven, and we eagerly await a Savior from there, the Lord Jesus Christ, who, by the power that enables Him to subject all things to Himself, will transform our lowly bodies to be like His glorious body (Phil. 3:20-21 Berean Standard Bible).

To the Ephesians:
Therefore you are no longer strangers and foreigners, but fellow citizens with the saints and members of God's household (Ephesians 2:19 BSB).

But he also noted the Christian responsibilities to the temporal kingdom within which they live.

To the Romans:
Everyone must submit himself to the governing authorities, for there is no authority except that which is from God...Therefore it is necessary to submit to authority, not only to avoid punishment, but also as a matter of conscience (see Rms. 13:1-7).

Peter also addressed the issue:
Submit yourselves for the Lord's sake to every human institution, whether to the king as the supreme authority, or to governors as those sent by him to punish those who do wrong and to praise those

who do right. For it is God's will that by doing good you should si-lence the ignorance of foolish men.

Live in freedom, but do not use your freedom as a cover-up for evil; live as servants of God. Treat everyone with high regard: Love the brotherhood of believers, fear God, honor the king (see 1 Pet. 2: 11-17 BSB).

Regardless of Government—Tyranny or Republic

When Paul and Peter gave the early Christians their directives about submission to the king, the Roman Empire was in charge of the world in which the Church was birthed. The emperor was the sole monarch. His word was law. The emperors were of unquestioned authority with unrestricted power. A thumbs-up meant life. A thumbs-down meant death. Regardless of the morality or lack of morality that guided them.

Paul and Peter urged the early Christians to submit to the state. They themselves provided models by submitting to that authority. In the end, both would die as martyrs in Rome. Paul, as a Roman citizen, was likely beheaded. Peter, not being a Roman citizen, was crucified. He requested to be crucified upside down because he felt unworthy of being crucified in the same manner as his Lord. Both men felt the tyranny of Rome.

But in 18th century America, when the yoke of tyranny was thrown off during the revolution, a different form of government emerged. It was informed by the Greeks, the Romans, and English common law. It was founded upon Judeo-Christian principles. It was a federal constitutional Republic. When Benjamin Franklin was asked what they had arrived at, he responded, "A republic, if you can keep it."

Franklin knew that a republic form of government required the active participation of the citizens.

Abraham Lincoln addressed the nature of the government of the United States in the Gettysburg Address. He stated the nature of our

Republic in the last ringing words of his brief address.

"It is rather for us to be here dedicated to the great task remaining before us, that from these honored dead we take increased devotion to that cause for which they gave the last full measure of devotion, that we here highly resolve that these dead shall not have died in vain, that this nation, under God, shall have a new birth of freedom, and that government of the people, by the people, for the people, shall not perish from the earth."

We are a nation *of*, *by*, and *for* the people. That places certain demands upon us. That means we must participate. How? Here are a few essential requirements.

Educate

An informed citizenry is absolutely indispensable to the American republic. *George Washington* said this in his farewell address:

"It is substantially true that virtue or morality is a necessary spring of popular government. The rule, indeed, extends with more or less force to every species of free government. Who that is a sincere friend to it can look with indifference upon attempts to shake the foundation of the fabric?

"Promote then, as an object of primary importance, institutions for the general diffusion of knowledge. In proportion as the structure of a government gives force to public opinion, it is essential that public opinion should be enlightened."

Washington maintained that the continuation of the Republic is dependent upon the morality and education of the general public.

John Adams said the same thing. "We cannot have an ignorant citizenry and maintain for long our form of government." Adams was a proponent of education for "every rank and class of people, down to the lowest and the poorest." Its importance required that "no expense...would be too extravagant."

Thomas Jefferson believed in a system ruled by the people at the local level. For that to be effective, an educated citizenry was required. He emphasized reading, writing, and arithmetic for everyone. Further education needed to focus on history and the social sciences. Jefferson believed that in order for a society to be self-governed, it had to be educated and free-thinking.

We must invest the time to educate ourselves on the issues facing our nation. Put in the time. Find solid sources. Prepare your mind.

Engage

God's purpose is being worked out regardless of who is on the throne. But we do not withdraw from a system of government that allows for and was structured for the protection and freedom of its citizens to practice their faith in the public square. We cannot—must not—withdraw. We must engage.

That system is under attack in the most diabolic ways from all quarters. And we are called to yield no quarter. We engage our minds, our hearts, and our souls in the fight. And make no mistake, the battle we engage is a spiritual battle.

What does it take for evil to win? Nothing more than for good people to remain silent.

During the 2012 election for instance, 30 million Christians sat it out. They did not vote. In the 2020 election, 6 - 7% of the evangelical community sat on their ballots. And look at the state of the country in just under three years.

And yes, we know that it did not get in the condition in these few years. People of both parties have participated in pushing the United States to the brink of the abyss. They are all friends, move in the same circles.

Look at who the outsiders are. Look at who they fear more than anyone else. A wrench was thrown in their well-oiled machine by outsiders. The tide was being turned back. Progress was being made. But it was not a progress that the elites who run this system wanted. What did it take for a political victory to turn the world around to go in a downward spiral? Good people to remain silent.

If we are to change the culture, we must engage the culture.

We are in more danger of losing this form of government and the freedoms it promises than at any time since the struggle in the Revolution that gave birth to it. Danger even greater than the Civil War. Abraham Lincoln's words of concern should resonate in every heart— "Now we are engaged in a great civil war, testing whether that nation, or any nation so conceived and so dedicated, can long endure." Shall we endure? If so, engage.

Enlist

Others must be enlisted in the ranks of concerned, engaged patriots. It is up to each of us to spread the word. Others must be brought to the war. Family, friends, work associates, other Christian citizens, all who profess love for this nation.

Lincoln again challenges us—"that this nation, under God, shall have a new birth of freedom, and that government *of the people, by the people, for the people*, shall not perish from the earth."

Christian canaries, Paul and Peter, urge us—Arise! Stand firm! Do not yield! Regardless of the cost.

Steps to take now:

Action # 1: Identify sources of reliable information to continue educating yourself on the issues that are confronting our personal lives, our faith, and our nation.

Action # 2: Visit https://ballotpedia.org. Ballotpedia is the digital encyclopedia of American politics and elections seeking to inform people about politics by providing accurate and objective information. A good place to begin exploration.

Chapter Four
A Nation Under Supernatural Discipline

At least two dimensions exist in our world. First is the plane we see with our *physical eyes*. That's an easy one. We watch our children and grandchildren play and grow before our eyes. We view beautiful sunsets and equally magnificent sunrises. All of us (who have physical vision) have the capacity to view and admire the physical beauty of our world. One of our authors lives in the Northern Rockies in Montana. It is a place of immense beauty. That beauty nurtures the soul and inspires awe of God the Creator.

However, our physical vision also sees injustices, crimes, man's inhumanity to man, and the results of a rebellious nature everywhere we turn. As much as we want to be insulated from it, we cannot avoid the fact that some people in our culture are forced to choose between eating and purchasing needed medicines.

Nearly a century has passed since the Great Depression that began with the stock market collapse of 1929. During the decade-long financial struggle, shantytowns appeared across America as unemployed people were evicted from their homes. Farmers had their farms foreclosed upon, leaving them as sharecroppers. Men sought work and no work was to be found. Mothers struggled to feed their families.

As the Depression worsened, citizens began to look toward the Federal government for assistance. When the government failed to provide relief, President Hubert Hoover was blamed for the economic and social conditions of the nation. The shantytowns that cropped up became known as "Hoovervilles."

It's about here that reasonably thinking people would have Santayana's words—*Those who cannot remember the past are condemned to repeat it*—ringing in their ears. One hundred years ago shantytowns dotted the landscape of America. Today, it's tent cities. It seems that about every American metropolis is struggling to execute an effective plan to eradicate the dilemma of homelessness, the blight of drug addiction, and the plight of desperate people living at our doorsteps. Whole downtown centers are being hollowed out as businesses close their doors and flee the decay and degradation.

To no avail.

Yes, our world is a beautiful place, but it's a proverbial house of horrors too.

Spiritual Warfare

Angels and Demons is a popular game played with a group numbering 6 – 25 players. Each player is given a role combination defining their faction. The game is set in Foix, a small town that has a castle which has withstood weather and warriors for centuries. Little do the townspeople realize that they will be a part of an ongoing battle between two epic forces. Angels and demons disguise themselves in human form. The crux of the game is this: will demons raze the town, leaving a trail of disaster and devastation, or will angels draw out the good in the town leaving only a barren landscape? Can the townsfolk of Foix hold onto everything they hold dear?

In our very real world, another plane of warfare is operating simultaneously with what we experience physically. An unseen, supernatural dimension exists that can only be viewed with *spiritual eyes*. It is important to understand that every issue our culture faces is being influenced by undeniable spiritual forces. Whether we recognize it, believe it, or acknowledge it, two forces are battling for the soul of our nation. *Angels and Demons* is a game. But unseen cosmic forces around us are not playing a game.

64

And these cosmic forces are active right now.

In a day when "follow the science" is a failing solution for the social and moral ills of a nation, it is time to look beyond ourselves and understand that the world we see physically is temporal, while the world we can only view spiritually is authentic and trustworthy. Tragically, science is tuned into believing only what can be seen and measured is real. Science is incapable of wrapping its mind around the fact an unseen world is the arena for cosmic conflict. As in any battle, two opposing supernatural bodies are perpetually clashing. Can these two combatants be identified? Yes. They can and have been since the inception of humanity.

Angelic Forces of Light

Angels are supernatural beings who the late Billy Graham tagged as "God's secret agents." It would be wise to reject typical views our culture holds about angels. One such image is an angel sitting on a cloud plucking a harp. Others tout the notion that angels are babies. Cherubs are depicted as small angelic beings with wings. You may have seen the infant icons in a garden center or outdoor furniture business. This image is faulty at its core because it presents angels as being mythologically weak, emaciated, or feministic beings.

Angels are not "melba toast" creatures. Cherubs are fierce warriors unmatched by any force known to man. Angels, like Scotch® tape, cannot be seen, but we know they are there. Our physical eyes are not designed to see angels any more than we can see an electric current flowing along the wiring in our homes. Our ability to recognize reality has boundaries. For instance, Monarch butterflies possess an incredible guidance system tapping a broader, unseen world.

Just like we cannot understand the migration of butterflies, we cannot fathom the fact that angels are present and in our presence. Here is how Graham described these messengers of the Most High.

"They warn of God's impending judgment; they spell out the tenderness of His love; they meet a desperate need; then they are gone. Of one thing we can be sure: angels never draw attention to themselves but ascribe glory to God and press His message upon the hearers as a delivering and sustaining word of the highest order." *(Angels: God's Secret Agents)*

Recognizing these unseen creatures is not foreign to mankind's history. The ancient Egyptians made tombs for their dead more impregnable and lavish than their homes because they believed angels would visit them in ages to come. Followers of Islam believe that at least two angels are assigned to each person. One angel records the good works while another angel notes the evil.

Historically the most trustworthy reference to angels is found in the 66 books comprising the Bible.

Angels are mentioned directly or indirectly approximately 300 times in biblical texts which give us a better understanding of the mighty power of these supernatural beings. It's in Psalm 68:17 where David noted their vast number at 20,000. Tens of thousands of angels attended the moment when God gave Moses the Law (Deuteronomy 33:2).

During the ministry days of Jesus, Roman legions were commonplace. A typical legion numbered to 5,000 soldiers. According to Matthew 26:53, Jesus could have called 12 legions of angels (60,000) to deliver Him from the cross.

These supernatural beings are ever-present in times of need. You might recall the Old Testament encounter in 2 Kings 6. Ben-Hadad, king of Syria, sought to eliminate Elisha by sending a great army to capture him. The servant of Elisha arose early and went out of the house. To his dismay and horror, he saw the numerous horses and chariots of Ben-Hadad. He and his master were surrounded on all sides. In panic, he asked the prophet, "What shall we do?"

Elisha replied, *"Do not be afraid, for those who are with us are more than those who are with them."* Then Elisha prayed and said, *"O Lord, please open his eyes that he may see."* So the Lord opened the eyes of the young man, and he saw, and behold, the mountain *was full of horses and chariots of fire all around Elisha* (2 Kings 6:16-17).

The enemies of the man of God were of one plane, the physical. The army of the Lord were of another plane, the spiritual. The army of the enemy of the people of God were blinded, taken into the presence of their enemy in Samaria, soundly defeated and humiliated in their defeat at the hands of a mightier spiritual force.

Angelic strength is unmatched, unparalleled, and amazingly available to any person or nation that recognizes their presence.

Sadly, a symptom of a culture in free-fall is that it neglects the notion of the spiritual plane. By dismissing this idea, we are rejecting the concept of an invisible world with greater power than this world will ever possess. Michael Heiser calls this the *Unseen Realm*. This realm is just as real, or even more so, than the physical world we inhabit.

Demonic Forces of Darkness

Another set of combatants on this spiritual plane is also powerful, subtle, and unrelenting with their attack on our world and especially (as we are concerned) on our nation. We are witnessing a culture that is falling deeper and deeper into various deviant lifestyles of debauchery. Perversion of that which is good is a stock-in-trade tactic. The words of Jesus describe this enemy as a *thief* (who) *comes only to steal and kill and destroy.* Since the birth of America in 1776, the Adversary and his minions have had our nation in a systematic downward spiral. Here are a few examples of his devilish efforts.

In their case the god of this world has blinded the minds of the unbelievers. (2 Cor. 4:4)

Be sober-minded, be watchful. Your adversary the devil prowls around like a roaring lion seeking someone to devour. Resist him... (1 Peter 5:8 – 9a)

Do not foolishly believe the devil operates alone. No, he has forces of darkness at his bidding. Ephesians 6:10 – 13 outlines the battles we face with supernatural adversaries. Note especially the list of opposing forces Paul lists in this passage:

Finally, be strong in the Lord and in the strength of his might. Put on the whole armor of God, that you may be able to stand against the schemes of the devil. For we do not wrestle against flesh and blood, but against the rulers, against the authorities, against the cosmic powers over this present darkness, against the spiritual forces of evil in the heavenly places. Therefore, take up the whole armor of God, that you may be able to withstand in the evil day, and having done all, to stand firm.

This is no game. Our nation is in a hand-to-hand, face-to-face, life-and-death struggle for our very way of life. Evil influences are present and growing daily throughout our culture. Here are a few illustrations of depravity and its slippery slide.

- There is a swift movement afoot for creating a reliable Artificial Intelligence.
- Our nation is on the verge of financial bankruptcy with over 34 (nearly 35) trillion dollars of unstainable debt. Many economists believe unfunded mandates exceed 100 trillion dollars.
- Rejection of fundamental authority is unleashing hell on our city streets.
- Trustworthy authority is being replaced by a seared conscience of reprobate minds.
- Our government is stagnant. Statesmen and stateswomen are needed, not politicians.
- The issue of gender identity is being allowed more exposure creating confusion at deeper levels for our children. We do not grasp the damages occurring with this evil.

One of the devil's traps is to divert our thinking from the help God offers us in our struggles against the forces of evil. Like the servant of Elisha, our eyes cannot see the forces arrayed on our behalf.

We are not alone in this supernatural battle. We are not fighting a losing battle. However, we would be wise to recognize the cosmic forces of darkness that are in operation within our culture. And while we might be the ultimate victors as the army of God, that does not mean that our nation will emerge unscathed. The nation might not even survive.

We are being deceived to believe our enemy has an "R" or "D" attached to their names. Terms of derision like "racist," "bigot," and "radical" permeate the conversation of an agenda-driven media. We must never forget that the Adversary seeks to marginalize our nation by dividing it from within. If we are fighting each other, attention is taken off him. Notice how Paul describes these foes:

1. This evil influence includes *"the cosmic powers over this present darkness."* Maybe this is the highest operation of this supernatural enemy.

2. This evil influence encompasses, *"the rulers, the authorities."* It's possible that these demons infiltrate the political arena. Surely, we have witnessed demonic work in action through various world leaders including Russia's Vladimir Putin, China's Xi Jinping, and North Korea's Kim Jong Un. It is feared (but not surprising) that wicked leadership has permeated the United States government too.

3. This evil influence is *"spiritual forces of evil in the heavenly places."* These vile, wretched, deplorable spirits go about doing whatever they can to tempt us into deeper depravity as a culture. What do we do in times of spiritual attack? We are called simply to "stand."

That's what a sentinel does. He stands. She steps up in crucial moments. Like the steely-eyed commitment of a Tomb Guard who willingly takes his watch, we too are to be found standing. How do we overcome the forces of darkness that have such deep roots in our culture? Consider the insight of 2 Corinthians 10:4-5:

> *For the weapons of our warfare are not of the flesh but have divine power to destroy strongholds. We destroy arguments and every lofty opinion raised against the knowledge of God, and take every thought captive to obey Christ...*

No wise sentinel would enter a cosmic battle without being equipped with supernatural weaponry. Sounding an alarm demands courage and resolve. It is feared that reasonably thinking people have chosen to be silent too long. So long, that a vocal minority has been tolerated and coddled without challenge. It seems this deviant sector of our culture has invaded the marketplace of thought to manipulate the silent majority.

The voices of the media are arrayed against the forces of light and it is a message filled with darkness. The message is so similar that the source no longer matters. Listen to the rhetoric that comes from the media, regardless of the form or source. The identical script is being used. The media is nothing more than propaganda mills. And their craven message is working.

It's time to stand. It's time to speak up and speak out against every lofty thing that exalts itself against the knowledge of God.

Empires and Nations Come and Go

Recognizing the supernatural battle that is raging in our culture must become a priority if we are to survive as a nation. Our times resemble those in the days of Noah where God said,

> *"My Spirit shall not always strive with man..."* --Genesis 6:3a

Though our nation has been blessed throughout our history, lessons are to be learned from empires and nations that refused to remain in an intimate relationship with the Lord. Reserved in the dust of the past are empires such as: Assyrian, Persian, Greek, Roman, Egyptian, Mongolian, Incan, Spanish, and British.

It seems that God uses empires to bring discipline to those He treasures. Such was true with the chosen people of God, the Israelites. The tribe of Abraham was chosen as an instrument of God's plan of redemption. It would be through them that God would send the Messiah, the Redeemer. He chose them, formed them into a nation, and gave them a particular piece of critical real estate. And at the exact, optimum moment God sent His son through the lineage of Abraham: *But when the fullness of time had come, God sent forth his Son, born of woman, born under the law, to redeem those who were under the law, so that we might receive adoption as sons.* (Galatians 4:4-5).

After the reign of Solomon, the nation of Israel split into two different kingdoms. First was the Northern Kingdom (Israel) comprised of ten tribes. Second was the Southern Kingdom (Judah), comprised of two tribes. Because He cared for His promised people, God sent sentinels into their midst. These sentinels were called prophets. Their message was a warning of God's impending judgment. Men who prophesied to the Northern Kingdom were Elijah, Elisha, Amos and Hosea. Southern Kingdom sentinels were Isaiah, Joel, Micah, Zephaniah, and Habakkuk.

Whether Northern or Southern Kingdom, the message from the Lord was a call to repentance. But the people of God, those who had been blessed for centuries, had now developed a hardened heart against the Lord. Consider the message of Amos. Speaking to his audience in a geographically, counter-clockwise fashion, Amos faithfully called every neighbor of Israel to repentance. Damascus, Gaza, Tyre, Edom, Ammonites, Moab, and finally...Judah.

Ripped from the Headlines
The prophecy of Amos is like reading a current issue of the *Wall Street Journal*. The failures of Israel have stark resemblance to our culture.

- Carnal security...guilty
- Scoffing at God's judgment...guilty
- Known for their violence and oppression of poor...guilty
- Laziness...guilty
- Idle pleasures including drunkenness...guilty
- Lack of compassion...guilty

God's swift judgment on the Northern Kingdom came at the hands of the Assyrians in 722 B.C. These oppressors were known for taking captives, dispersing, and absorbing them into their own culture.

Larry Garner summarizes: "It was this practice that eliminated the Northern Kingdom of Israel from history. A dispersed people cannot unify. Eventually, they lose their history and identity."

The parallels of the Northern Kingdom's demise and that of our present-day culture are alarming. It is imperative that we remember those eight factors that individually or in combination have caused empires and nations to collapse.

- They are conquered by an external enemy.
- They debase their currency, destroy their economy and go bankrupt.
- They do not manage succession of power.
- They are ruled by incompetent leaders and crater from the inside.
- They create or fall prey to an ecological catastrophe.
- They lose belief in themselves. They destroy imagery from the past.
- They decay morally and ethically.
- They over-extend their resources.

And there are others. For instance, some destroy their own future generations, sacrificing their own children. Some attack and destroy the nuclear family, the very basis of all civilization. Some break apart in civil war, attacking and ripping the fabric of their own culture. Some allow their own population to be displaced and replaced by unchecked immigration, in effect, an invasion of their country.

Reading the prophets and this list of causes of empire collapse is like watching a news reporter describe our culture today. But our culture does not have to go the way of fallen empires or nations. There is a better way. There is time to reverse direction and change our ways.

Some of us fear God's hand will be placed on our culture in judgment; a greater fear is that God's hand is removed from it. It's time to stand, before God's hand of blessing is removed from us.

Billy Graham called Psalm 106:15 the most terrifying verse in the Bible—*he gave them what they asked, but sent a wasting disease among them.* What if God simply gave us what we want—what we choose? Is that not a terrifying thought?

C.S. Lewis captured the exact same thought as did Billy Graham. Allow his words to penetrate your heart:

"There are only two kinds of people in the end: those who say to God, 'Thy will be done' and those to whom God says in the end, 'Thy will be done.' All that are in hell choose it. Without self-choice there could be no hell."

The prophet Joel describes the day of judgment as multitudes in the Valley of Decision. His language of judgment is vivid:

Put in the sickle,
for the harvest is ripe.
Go in, tread,
for the winepress is full.
The vats overflow,
for their evil is great.
Multitudes, multitudes,
in the valley of decision!

For the day of the Lord is near
in the valley of decision.

Joel 3:13-14

The winepress is full. We have stored up wickedness against the Lord. Judgment is near in the Valley of Decision.

We are in a day of choosing. What shall we choose?

Steps to take now:

Action # 1: Pray for wisdom in seeking information. So many voices clamor for our attention. We need to be wise in where we spend our time and to which voices we listen.

Action # 2: Visit the Center for Security Policy (https://centerforsecuritypolicy.org). Explore their site to discover topics that can help educate you about policies to protect our future. Their mission is to secure America's founding principles and freedom through forthright national security analysis and policy solutions.

Action # 3: Identify the top two or three concerns for you. As issues of concern arise before Congress, contact your appropriate congress members to express your wishes and opinions. They do, after all, work for us.

Action # 4: Contact your representatives and insist that our military leaders remove "sensitivity training" from every branch of military service.

Chapter Five
The Insanity of Fiscal Irresponsibility

Congratulations!

Canaries, welcome to debt that we did not sign a note to secure. As of May 1, 2023, the U.S. Treasury's official figure for debt equates to $93,988.00 per person living in the United States. Every household owes $239,763.00 dollars. Do you feel like celebrating?

Instead of seeking opinions from taxpayers, Washington bureaucrats continue to intrude into our lives and steal our livelihoods. This is blatant, deliberate theft. These elites have been doing this so long that they do not even wear pantyhose on their heads when they rob us. Instead, they rush to the nearest microphone and camera to brag about how they have passed monstrous omnibus bills chocked full of spending. They are proud of spending money we do not have. Putting the taxpayers on the hook for trillions of dollars.

And do not think this is one party over another. This trough has all the hogs of every stripe feeding at it. This issue more than any other reveals the Uni-party. They pretend to be offended by the foot-dragging of others. But they fool nobody. We know their game and we are tired of the blatant disdain with which they hold us. A basic civics lesson would do all of us good.

Basic Civics

Do you remember when civics was part of the curriculum of every public school in our nation? Until the 1960's, American adolescents were required to pass three separate courses in civics and government. However, civic offerings were removed as curriculum shifted to compensate for "core subjects" under the NCLB (No Child Left Behind) mandates that standardized testing regimes.

When civics was required in schools, young men and women readying to embark into an exciting future would grasp something of how their government operated. And they were aware of what their responsibilities were under our form of government.

We learned there were three branches of the federal government:

- *The Executive Branch:* The Office of the President of the United States
- *The Judicial Branch:* The Supreme Court
- *The Legislative Branch:* Comprised of two chambers—the Senate and the House of Representatives.

When it comes to spending, the Executive Branch is tasked with managing funds that the government receives. The Legislative Branch is responsible for developing the budget and allocating funds. The brilliance of the framers of our Constitution was how they utilized the separation of powers for a reason.

No single branch of government was to overreach into the commission of the other two branches. Changing this mindset meant changing minds. That meant changing the education of Americans. This subtle shift began when civics was jettisoned from education. The result is more than 50 years of students graduating from our schools who have no idea how government works.

The result is generations growing up in a culture of dependency on the government, or worse, have become our elected officials in Congress today. Sadly, too many of these politicians might not have a firm grasp on reality when it comes to spending.

Do these politicians understand the difficulty of creating a dollar? Just one dollar? Do they sign the front or the back of a pay check?

- The public sector (federal government, in this instance) has perfected the art of signing the back of checks, which means the federal government NEVER creates a dollar. It collects it through taxation and borrowing from lenders.
- The private sector (business) is the economic engine of our culture. The willingness to risk, struggle, save, and invest creates tax revenues for federal, state, and local governments.

Shockingly, it is the 33 million small firms (companies with less than 500 employees) which account for most businesses in America. These businesses are the primary job creators in America. The private sector includes "mom and pop" stores on the corner of every American neighborhood. These patriots with their businesses and their employees are the life blood of our economy.

Simply stated, the public sector spends money while the private sector creates money.

Denial

Generational ignorance as to how government operates has become a cultural norm. Ask the average person on the street about how the government works and you will get a stuttering, stammering response or a blank stare and silence. However, like giving car keys to an irresponsible driver or a credit card to a kid, the blame for allowing our country to fall into the fiscal disarray we are facing is OUR OWN FAULT.

It is feared that economically, we have allowed our governmental officials to thrive in a fantasy world where they spend Monopoly® dollars at alarming rates. To see how reckless the spending is, look at the National Debt Clock (https://usdebtclock.org). It is stunning how fast the digits flash through the windows. You can't watch it long without getting sick. Those are your dollars zipping by your eyes. They are coming out of your pocket or, more alarmingly, out of your children's or grandchildren's pockets. We are watching in real time our future of serfdom being revealed.

Our government representatives and officials (the unelected bureaucrats) live in Beltway *denial* and have no idea, nor do they care, how common every-day, tax-paying Americans struggle day-to -day economically.

"Denial is not a river in Egypt."

Denial is probably too nice a word for the theft and destruction that is occurring. Just look at the reckless attitude toward our national debt. When you go to the National Debt Clock, you will see the debt is measured in trillions of dollars. We seem to have blown right by the "billion" term. That's just so yesterday! Politicians address nearly everything in terms of trillions now.

What does a trillion dollars look like? Here is an attempt to get your mind around that amount— it's a million millions; one thousand billions; one followed by 12 zeros. If a trillion dollars were laid end to end, the line would stretch 96,906,656 miles, a distance farther than our sun is from the earth. As of January 2023, six out of ten adults are living paycheck to paycheck. But, let's set that aside for a moment—suppose your household had one trillion dollars to simply blow away. Let this sink in for a moment. If your family spent $40 dollars per second, it would take 792.5 years to go broke.

Our nation is awash with an unsustainable debt. Today, our national debt is nearing 35 trillion dollars (and counting faster than you can imagine). That is almost three times the annual revenues collected by all the world governments combined! Also, there is an elephant in the room. A BIG one. We are told to ignore our unfunded mandates. These unfunded liabilities include promised Social Security, Medicare, and government pensions that Washington will not have the money to pay. Some leading economists believe the federal government really owes north of 100 trillion dollars.

Like a television commercial that promises, "But wait, there's more." Because of ignorance or indifference, the American citizen-

78

ry does not realize the rate of spending by our federal government. At present, our politicians plan to spend (at current spending rates) more than 6 trillion dollars annually. And they would spend more. Which they probably will. Deficits as far as the eye can see.

We do not bring in that much money in a year. We are in continual deficit spending. In FY 2022, the federal government spent $6.5 trillion. We are living on borrowed money and borrowed time.

The latest economic statistics show that 60 percent of American families have less than $1000 dollars available in case of an emergency. Like most of the struggling families dotting the landscape of our nation, the federal government is broke.

There is a difference between being poor and being broke. Poverty occurs when someone has no money. Someone who is broke habitually wastes money, has none, and owes more than is possible for them to repay. That's broke. What's beyond broke? Whatever it is, that's what we are.

Read that again. We are broke. We are a debtor nation. We owe ourselves (we owe the Social Security system over 2.7 trillion dollars—remember that lock-box, it's filled with I-Owe-Yous), nations around the world (sovereign funds), we owe banks and businesses, we owe the Federal Reserve. You name the entity and someone is holding American debt.

And do you know who holds the bag on that debt? We do. The taxpayers. The people who can't put together a $1,000 in case of an emergency. We owe $93,988.00 per person. You'd think that owing that much money would make one feel wealthy. For truly, only the wealthy can carry debt like that.

Disaster

Over the last 40+ years the federal debt has grown at an average annual rate of 8.2% which accelerated from 10 trillion dollars to a whopping $34.6 trillion currently. (As of 3/28/2024, 8:56 AM, the amount we owe is $34,606,445,595,342.) And when you read this, it will be even higher. With the recent debt ceiling negotiation, we are projected to owe $36 trillion (or more) by January 1, 2025. Nobody is pumping the brakes. They are not attempting to slow the Debt Train. They have taken their hands off the throttle, off the brakes, and are in the dinning car having drinks on us. All the while derailment is coming. Here's what a disaster looks like—

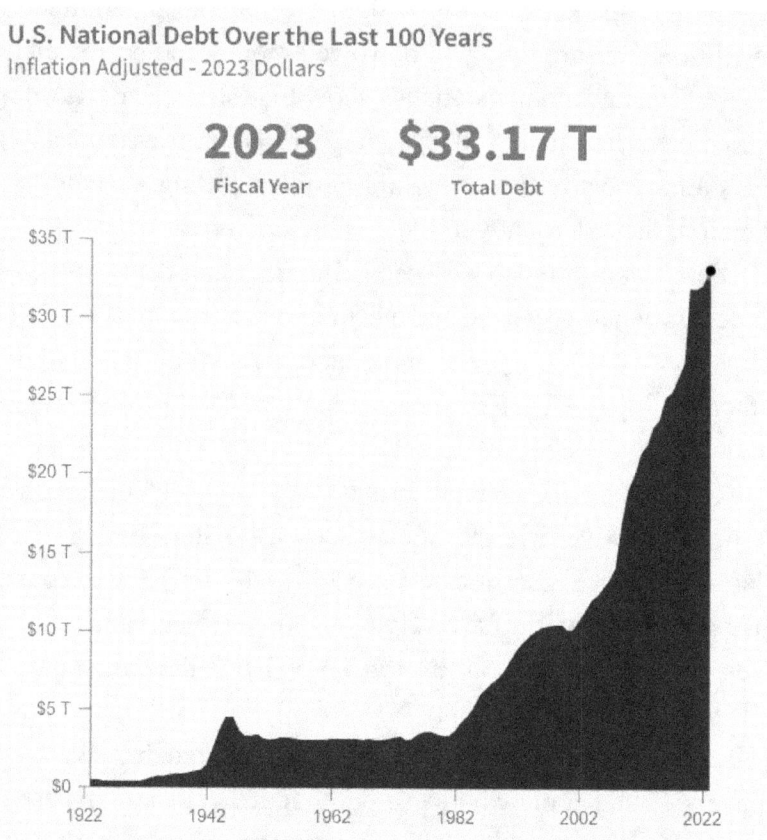

U.S. National Debt Over the Last 100 Years
Inflation Adjusted - 2023 Dollars

2023   **$33.17 T**
Fiscal Year   Total Debt

Visit the Historical Debt Outstanding dataset to explore and download this data. The inflation data is sourced from the Bureau of Labor Statistics.

Last Updated: September 30, 2023

This chart shows our debt spending for the last 100 years. A few observations are easy to make:

- During the 1920s borrowing was relatively tame.
- Then, the Depression hit, pushing borrowing higher throughout the 1930's.

- World War II hiked the debt noticeably and understandably.

- Debt spending remained fairly constant from 1950 until 1982.

- Then, the chart begins to climb and climb. Why? We went off the gold standard in 1971. We have been spending fiat currency—paper with nothing backing it but the "full faith and credit of the United States." For those who might wonder where that comes from, it comes from the U.S. taxpayers. We are on the hook for that debt.

And just to be on point—the chart is not that old but it is out of date. Frankly, we cannot keep up with the national debt. Take a pen and mark on the chart $34.6 trillion as of 3/28/2024. But by the time you mark the chart, it is out of date. Allow a reminder—go to https://www.usdebtclock.org. Be prepared to be shocked. That's your money and your children's future that you are watching zip past. Keeping the chart current with the debt clock is impossible.

In FY 2022, we added 2 trillion dollars to our debt. Since the debacle of the "Debt Ceiling Negotiations" in June of 2023, in just five weeks, a trillion dollars was added to the national debt after that disastrous agreement was reached. Some economists project $4 trillion to be added by January 1, 2025. That's the "or more."

And this expectation might be wildly out of range. Ink was still wet on that budget ceiling agreement, when the Treasury announced that it would offer (this means *borrow*) $1.3 trillion in T-bills to get us through the rest of the year. That "year" was the fiscal year that ended on September 30, 2023. After that deadline, $1.6 trillion in T-bills was offered (borrowed) for the next 6 months. No end in sight!

Eventually debt can become so large that the borrower is unable to touch the principal. All one is able to do is pay the interest. We are rapidly approaching that threshold. This year the interest payment on the national debt will surpass the expenditures for the Department of Defense. (Some suggest our interest to top $1 trillion.)

The government is good at hiding what they are doing in the

labyrinth of the national budget. However, let's take them at their word for the sake of illustration (and alarm). According to the Department of Defense, "The FY 2023 DoD Budget request of $773.0 billion is a $30.7 billion, or 4.1% increase, from the FY 2022 enacted amount." (3/28/22) The Treasury Department has stated, "As of September 2023 it costs $879 billion to maintain the debt, which is 14% of the total federal spending. The national debt has increased every year over the past ten years." (https://fiscaldata.treasury.gov/americas-finance-guide/national-debt/)

When you have to borrow money to pay your interest on your borrowed money, you are in trouble. Disaster looms large.

Four Pockets

Where does our government get this kind of "extra" cash? The long arm of bureaucratic over-spending reaches into four pockets.

First is foreign loans. One of our leading lenders is China. A motive for Chinese lenders buying so many U.S. Treasury Securities is that they want the "yuan" currency attached to the American dollar.

China is an economic enemy of America. The insanity of our spending is that we borrow from an enemy, who in turn uses INTEREST payments to fill their war chests and stimulate their national economy. Our money has been the foundation of their growth to a global economic power. Amazingly, a move to replace the America dollar with another currency is afoot. The tenacles of their global influence has 24 nations agreeing to follow China's lead.

Anyone watching this global canary? By borrowing from China, we are funding our own destruction. That's national suicide.

A second pocket is Americans who purchase the same Treasury Securities. During World War II, war bonds were sold to support the cause for freedom and ultimate victory by Allied Forces led by American military personnel. Today, investing in T-Bills is a popular move among those without appetite for Wall Street volatility.

A third pocket is relying on the Federal Reserve. So that you know, the Federal Reserve is the group that "printed" all that currency. So, when the federal government needs more cash, the phone rings at the Federal Reserve which in turn obliges the request by authorizing the Bureau of Engraving and Printing to fire up the printing presses. Every twenty-four hours 541 million dollars are produced. And today, the printing presses are archaic. More for show. Because with a few mouse clicks, money is created out of thin air.

A fourth pocket is borrowing from government trust funds such as Social Security, the largest account to which the U.S. Treasury owes money. As of December 2022, the Social Security Administration is owed 2.7 trillion dollars by the federal government.

Unsustainable

October 1 through September 30 is the fiscal year of the federal government. During the first six months of fiscal year 2023, the federal government collected 2.69 trillion dollars in revenue but spent 3.61 trillion dollars.

In police work they call that a "clue."

The burn rate is unsustainable. We are currently borrowing a trillion dollars every 90 days. Look around. The canary is twitching in this financial cavern. How do we stop the bleeding? Remember the hard lesson: It's easy to run into debt. It's difficult to crawl out!

How might the voices of patriots be heard on this issue?

1. Call for a Balanced Budget Amendment in Federal Spending.

It's time to dust off the civics books and recall that public officials work for us. They do not operate in a vacuum; they should not be allowed to remain in echo chambers of the Beltway without accountability to those who sent them there. Just like crack addicts demand more cocaine, some of these politicians need incessant financial fixes to satisfy their spending habits.

Why would clear thinking people allow themselves to be led by financial children? Why do we continue to tolerate fiscal incompetence? Elections do have consequences.

In canary like fashion, John Adams, the second president of the United States, warned, "...liberty cannot be preserved without a general knowledge among the people..."

Liberty cannot be preserved without an informed citizenry. Adams stated that this informed citizenry is of more benefit to the welfare of the nation than all the property and wealth of the rich.

He went on to state that one of the more important items of knowledge is of the character and conduct of our representatives. And should those representatives fail to live up to the standards necessary to guide the nation, the informed citizenry has the right and the duty to select others who are better suited to the task of guiding the nation. (Papers of John Adams, volume 1, V. "A Dissertation on the Canon and the Feudal Law," No. 3)

Remember, democracy never lasts long. We do not have a democracy in history that did not commit suicide. The average age of constitutions (which is one gauge of political length of life) is around 17 years and that's across all countries since 1789 when our Constitution was implemented. The U.S. Constitution is the world's longest surviving written charter of government. Looks like we are the tallest midget in the parade—no offense intended. Constitutional democracies/republics find ways of dying at their own hands. They soon waste, exhaust, or murder themselves.

A balanced budget amendment simply calls for an immediate stop to fiscal irresponsibility. The federal government would not be allowed to spend one dollar more than the tax revenues received in that fiscal year. They have only two ways to balance its budget: raise taxes or reduce expenditures. The former is easy—contriving new taxes has become an art form by our politicians. A reduction in expenditures might be far more painful.

Prioritizing expenditures is difficult. Every hog wants their snout in the trough. If you've ever fed hogs, you know that they will run over you to get to the trough.

It's this kind of thinking that have the folks on Capitol Hill in a political corner. Raising taxes brings down the wrath of those who bear them and slashing entitlements or transferring benefits amount to political suicide. These Beltway hacks seem more interested in maintaining their power than doing the right thing for our culture, for our nation, and for our future.

Those of us who see the madness of our economic free fall must make our demands known to members of Congress before we reach the point of no return. One simple reason is unless we do, our grandchildren and great grandchildren will suffer the consequences of inaction by this generation of taxpayers.

A logical avenue might exist in solving this dilemma. It's basic economics called living within your means. Just like the typical family down the street (or maybe your family) cannot overspend, neither should our government be given a national checkbook and be able to spend money so recklessly. Curbing this kind of spending could be solved by introducing and passing legislation called "A Balanced Budget Amendment."

Discussion about this was birthed in the 1970's when it became apparent that the federal government was incapable of fiscal responsibility. Our politicians have been talking about it ever since. But as we all know, talk is cheap and delay is expensive. Advocates of the Constitutional amendment relish citing Thomas Jefferson, who just two years after the Constitution had been a proponent for a Constitutional amendment. He said—

> "I wish it were possible to obtain a single amendment to our Constitution. I would be willing to depend on that alone for the reduction of the administration of our government to the genuine principles of its Constitution; I mean an article, taking from the Federal government the power of borrowing."

Such a change would affect spending by drawing the federal budget closer to the flame of the framers of the Constitution. It would also address deficit spending. Politicians love to spend our money almost as much as our culture loves those spending programs. However, achieving the logical goal of getting our financial house in order will never be met until those recipients of federal dollars discontinue their expectations toward federal officials to haul in truckloads of Benjamins to their districts.

Several financial problems in America would be solved by balancing the federal budget. Yet at the same time, other problems would be created. By mandating spending limits on Capitol Hill, some politicians might advocate the need for additional government intervention and higher taxes.

Like Pavlov's dogs, our culture has been conditioned to expect (even demand) entitlements that benefit themselves. We want federal spending to be curbed but not where it impacts us. Why? Because Americans love their money. And it is the love of money which Paul identifies as the root of all evil: *For the love of money is a root of all kinds of evils. It is through this craving that some have wandered away from the faith and pierced themselves with many pangs* (1 Tim. 6:10).

The Theory of Going Broke

Deficit spending finds its roots in the Keynesian theory. John Maynard Keynes believed government spending and debt are factors in stimulating economic activity. He is the father of deficit spending. This British economist argued that demand drives supply and that healthy economies spend or invest more than they save.

A controversial side of the Keynesian theory concerns how the federal government finances its spending habits. Keynes believed the government should borrow money by selling treasury bonds. It should never attempt to balance its budget. Rather, run a deficit.

Politicians have been running with that idea ever since. This is an idea that puts feed in the trough for our pork-minded politicians. And, like too many of our public officials, were he alive today, Keynes would reject any call to a Constitutional change that affected federal spending patterns.

It's time for patriots to unite in calling for a Constitutional amendment that stops the insanity of careless spending by our federal officials.

2. Avoid pork barrel spending in Congress.

The phrase "pork barrel" was introduced to Congress in 1863. It referred to any monies a government spends on its citizens. Ten years later, the concept of pork-barrel politics had evolved to mean spending by a politician that benefited *certain* constituents in exchange for their support whether financial or at the ballot box. Scottish scholar, Alexander Frasier Tytler, brilliantly predicted:

> "A democracy cannot exist as a permanent form of government. It can only exist until the voters discover that they can vote themselves largesse from the public treasury. From that moment on, the majority always votes for the candidates promising the most benefits from the public treasury with the result that a democracy always collapses over loose financial policy, always followed by a dictatorship."

His haunting words continued to describe civilizations—

> "The average age of the world's greatest civilizations has been 200 years. These nations have progressed through this sequence:

- From bondage to spiritual faith;
- From spiritual faith to great courage;
- From great courage to liberty;
- From liberty to abundance;
- From abundance to selfishness;
- From selfishness to apathy;
- From apathy to dependence;
- From dependence back into bondage."

This cycle or sequence should send shivers down the spine of every American. Study it for a moment and pinpoint where our nation is.

If it looks like a duck, walks like a duck, and sounds like a duck—it's a duck. In short, savvy politicians have been using federal tax dollars that for all appearances seem to be a bribe to secure votes in an upcoming election.

Furthermore, this cycle is self-perpetuating. Politicians have perfected an art of directing funds to voters who in turn race to the ballot box to vote for politicians who will direct funds back to them. It's madness! What is tagged as pork-barrel expenditures? According to Citizens Against Government Waste, a project is "pork" when:

- Funds are requested by only one chamber of Congress.
- Funds are not specifically authorized nor competitively awarded.
- Funds are not subject to congressional hearings.
- The expenditure serves only a local or special interest.

An example of pork-barrel gimmicks is when one politician from one state who wants government funds for a specific project, like expanding the electrical grid to provide power to electric vehicles. The state receives hundreds of millions of dollars from the federal government which provides an economic boon to that state. The benefit of this investment (called "rent-seeking") remains within that state which means the other 49 states contribute to financing a project they cannot enjoy.

In recent years, "earmarking" became an expression of pork-barrel spending. It involves placing legislative additions on appropriation bills as a way to redirect federal funds to projects near and dear to the heart of citizens (at least for some of those citizens) of the lawmaker's state.

An example of a potential earmark boondoggle was called, "A Bridge to Nowhere." This was a 200-million-dollar expenditure that proposed building a bridge from mainland Alaska to an island of only 50 inhabitants. Fortunately, the project was defeated.

In 2021, "Community Project Funding" was introduced by

House Democrats to revive earmarks. The rules were that earmarks would be limited to 1% of discretionary funding and no lawmaker could submit more than ten funding requests per budget year. This change would allow both parties to receive credit for funding local projects. In 2021, 285 such projects were identified at a total cost of 16.8 billion dollars. Earmarks border on insanity.

A Balanced-Budget Amendment coupled with discontinuing "Community Project Funding" might begin to turn the tide away from financial disaster that is looming. Implementing a federal flat tax (where everyone pays taxes) and removing the unapproved and unappropriated discretionary spending called, "Executive Orders," would put a lid on federal waste too. (And we are aware that each of these orders has positive and negative consequences. Each should be weighed to see if the benefits outweigh the negative impacts.)

3. Initiate term limits for federally elected officials.

Federal politicians are elected to their respective seats. Members of the House of Representatives are elected for two years while Senate members sit for six years. The offices of the President and Vice President are four-year terms. An unaddressed problem is being perpetuated by allowing these officials to remain in office for YEARS and YEARS.

Only the office of President and Vice-President are term limited. And that was only after the extended run of Franklin D. Roosevelt. It is doubtful the framers of the Constitution envisioned career politicians who come to Washington and overstay their welcome.

The Congressional Research Service, has released a profile of the 118th Congress.

- The average age of Members of the House of Representatives is 57.9 years.
- The average length of service is 8.5 years;
- The average age of Senate members is 64.0 years and average years of service is 11.2 years.

Career politicians hide behind these "averages." Diane Feinstein was the oldest sitting U.S. senator and member of Congress. She was the longest-serving U.S. senator from California. Feinstein came to Washington in 1992. (During the editing of this book, Senator Feinstein died.) Before becoming the Vice President and now President, Joe Biden served for 36 years as a Senator from Delaware. Two Kentucky congressmen hold longevity terms—Mitch McConnell and Hal Rogers. McConnell at 38 years; Rogers at 42.

And when we dig into the history, Strom Thurmond was 100 years old while still in office and served 48 years as a senator. Robert Byrd, Daniel Inouye, and Patrick Leahy also camped out in Washington D.C. John Dingell, Jr. of Michigan holds the record for the longest consecutive years of service with more than 59 years. That's almost 30 elected terms to office.

The Founders did not imagine a professional political class. Between the professional political class and the permanent administrative class, the present government would be unrecognizable to those early patriots.

Like fish, too many of our federal politicians begin to smell after some time passes. They stay too long and accomplish too little. Thank them for their service and encourage them to become gainfully employed in the private sector as soon as possible. Why? One word—entitlement! They believe they are entitled to be there.

It is hoped that both Chambers are not filled with narcissists who believe the federal government cannot survive without them. But it is human nature to think more highly of ourselves than we should. The combination of narcissism and an entitlement mentality creates an atmosphere that fosters government financial waste.

Consider "entitled narcissistic politicians" for a moment. Like New York's 3rd District's Republican Representative, George Santos. The 34-year old Santos was the first openly gay representative who supported LGBTQ rights. (Which stands for lesbian, gay, bisexual, transgender, queer. But some people say that LGBTQ stands for "*Let's Get Biden To Quit*.") Santos' campaign slogan was "Save the American Dream." However, the people he represented learned that he lied about his entire resume.

He touted having studied at Baruch College and New York University; he claimed to have been a Wall Street success working with Citigroup and Goldman Sachs; he boasted of owning several pieces of real estate as rental properties. Yet, when pressed, Santos admitted all were fabrications (a longer word than *lies*). Why is honesty such an important quality for elected officials?

Our elected representatives should be people of integrity. Integrity is at the root of every decision people make. Santos became one of our national leaders by weaving a fabric of lies. His dishonesty could have compromised national security and federal leadership. He could not be trusted and could not be allowed to represent the American public in any capacity. He was expelled from the House of Representatives on December 1, 2023.

Our politicians must find a midpoint between longevity and effectiveness. How could Diane Feinstein continue to work at her advanced age and in such poor health? When the people of Pennsylvania elected John Fetterman, they had to be concerned. His health was fragile and imperiled. Yet, he was installed. And consider the deteriorating cognitive functions of President Joe Biden.

Whether it is long or short terms, these entitled, narcissistic politicians (and those who prop them up) represent a weakness to the enemies of our nation. Like retiring professional athletes, these government officials need to know when to go home.

May there be a new generation of canaries, who are ready to stand up in the dark mine of the Deep State and the corruption-riddled institutions throughout Washington D. C. Where are the canaries in Congress? When will statesmen and stateswomen speak up and become a voice for the very people who provide more than 4 trillion dollars in revenue annually to the Federal coffers.

The story of Rip Van Winkle is about a man who, in a drunken stupor, falls asleep in the Catskill Mountains. He awakens 20 years later to a very changed world. When will our leaders wake up? Do they sleep in a drunken stupor caused from a "governmental spending" elixir?

Our culture, our way of life is in the balance. Toxic spending by the federal government must be identified and irradicated. Every decision made by taxpaying citizens determines if we avoid passing on an economic disaster to our children and grandchildren. Anything short of dramatic changes in the spending practices of our government is insane. If we keep doing what we are doing, we are going to keep getting what we are getting. Maybe that's why insanity has been defined by some wag as "doing the same thing over and over and expecting a different result."

Our nation, including this bloated federal government saturated with financially intoxicated officials and a growing greedy populace, could take a lesson from one of the smallest creatures that roam the earth. Proverbs 6:6-11 highlights the example of the ant, noting that we are to:

- Be self-motivated
- Be wise
- Prepare
- Arise from sleep and get busy
- Because if not, poverty will come upon us like an armed robber.

Here's some wisdom that ant might propose: a Balanced Budget Amendment, avoid "pork barrel spending," initiate term limits for federally elected officials, and then call the hand being held by our federal employees.

4. Call the "debt ceiling/debt limit" bluff.

At some point, federal governmental waste must be handled like a school yard bully. They must be challenged with canary-like "in-your-face" apologetics. When it comes to curbing spending, our federal government plays the American public like a fiddle.

We have lived on the national credit card so long that running up the debt ceiling is not improv. It is choreographed as well as any dance routine you will ever see. They make Fred and Ginger or Michael Jackson with *Thriller* look like pikers just stumbling around.

The debt ceiling (our national credit card limit) deadline looms ahead of us every year. This doesn't sneak up on anyone. Like the opening night of the play, everyone gets in costume, make-up, lines have been memorized, props are prepared, the stage is set. Everyone is just waiting for the curtain to open.

And the opening night has been publicized far in advance. Media plays its part. As does Wall Street, the Federal Reserve, and the Treasury. They all begin wringing their collective hands. They wonder in print and on the airwaves whether the debt ceiling will be raised. Those in power are for it. The "loyal opposition" are against it. We enter tense negotiations. And everyone is on pins and needles wondering, "Will we raise the ceiling?"

The opening line of the play might come from the Secretary of the Treasury telling everyone that the "full faith and credit of the United States is at risk."

One of the senators might go to microphones and before the cameras noting that "we must pay our bills."

A representative tells us that "global markets will tumble if we do not raise the ceiling."

Whichever Presidential party is in power drags their feet. The other side presses the issue as the deadline approaches.

Maybe a short-term continuing resolution is passed to get us past the crisis, buying us more time to negotiate. Wall Street wrings its hands—"Markets are in danger."

Politicians with grave faces voice concern for all the "little people" who are dependent upon government checks. It could be the military, the senior citizens who need to go to the doctor, or the children who would not get their meals at the local indoctrination centers that we call schools. Heart-string-tugging stories are highlighted by the media. Interviews are done across the country.

Another deadline is set—usually right before Christmas. The pressure builds. And at the last minute, just before the last plane out of Reagan National, an agreement is reached. Our nation is saved. An omnibus bill, overloaded with pork-barrel projects, is passed.

Everyone in the Senate slaps one another on the backs: "We've done our work." The Uni-party pops the corks on the champagne. And the tab for the party is given to the poor suckers who aren't even invited for a glass of water.

Did you feel that extra load of debt they put on you?

They think they are so slick. They think we are unaware. Or, too numb or dumb to care. They are wrong. This routine is so obvious. Does Christmas Day ever "sneak up" on you? Not likely! Retailers are decking the halls as early as Labor Day. It's not a surprise to merchants or consumers. There is a well-planned effort to compete for business.

The federal government is not a business. It is a public sector operation that is in a nosedive and our citizenry is riding the plane. Do these politicians really want to cut spending? Why do they collectively wait until the nation is "forced" to raise the debt ceiling? Fear tactics are pressed into action creating planned panic that "avoids default" just like our Congress purported in May 2023. That this Congress waits until the last minute for voting on the debt ceiling is a travesty. Here are a few of the compromising points.

- An additional 80 billion dollars previously appropriated to the IRS to update its systems and enhance tax code enforcement by hiring thousands of new agents was reduced by 20 billion dollars.

- Low-income individuals must meet work requirements to qualify for food assistance programs.

- 50 - 70 billion dollars will be returned from unused COVID-19 funds.

- Student loan payments must resume.

The next planned "debt ceiling" panic is scheduled for early 2025. Maybe every federal politician could slip down to an office supply to purchase a 2024 calendar! Because we do not need to wait until 2025 to address the debt ceiling.

Our "negotiators" did us no favors in this last fiasco. They handed over to Joe Biden everything he wanted. The "honorable opposition" had to bite their tongues to keep from gloating. And why wouldn't they? The debt ceiling is not a fixed amount. It is a date. Two years from now. So the Uni-party can spend, spend, spend. And do not think that the appropriations dealings are going to be any better. More debt. More interest. Eventually, we will be paying interest only. With no hope of ever touching principal.

Welcome to serfdom.

In 1965, radio personality, Paul Harvey delivered an address entitled *Freedom to Chains*. Here is his spot-on warning from that address:

"Once upon a time there was a nation great and powerful and good. Few were suffering from the aftermath of war, from a depression. And then came upon the scene a leader, an idealist, self-confident, intolerant to criticism. A wise lady limited his early activities to combating the financial depression, nobody could argue with that, but in a while he began to regulate business and establish new rules to govern commerce and finance. Some of them in diametrical disagreement with the God-Made laws of supply and demand, but anybody who disagreed with those new rules was promptly fired.

"The new leader saw that under the old system of free enterprise landlords prospered, so he levied new taxes to take away their profits and destroy what he called the "Monopoly of Capital." To please laborers, he controlled prices. To win the favor of the farmers, he gave them loans and subsidies. The National Debt mounted, alarmingly. Whenever anybody tried to tell him "that governments, even as people, can go broke, when they spend beyond their incomes," he said "They just didn't understand deficit finance."

"Well, what do you say? Did he build on rock or on sand? I say on sand. For you see this was the story of Emperor Su Tung Po (Tsu Tong Phao) who led China to its doom more than a thousand years ago. I am satisfied with all my heart that if Uncle Sam ever does get whipped, here too, it will have been an Inside Job."

If Congress Got Paid Like the Rest of Us

The Constitution established two houses of Congress—a somewhat more aristocratic Senate and a House of Representatives that was supposed to be all about direct, grass-roots democracy.

As they saw it, the voters in every district would get together every other November, pick someone in their community they respected, and send him to Washington for a couple of years to vote for his (or her) neighbors' best interests and those of the nation. The Founding Fathers did not envision a professional political class.

A stint in Congress was not supposed to make you rich.

Six Dollars per Day

When the Constitution was ratified, members of Congress were to be paid six dollars a day and then only when they met.
(Source: Commentary by Jack Lessenberry, *Michigan Radio's political analyst*— https://www.michiganradio.org/opinion/2016-04-18/the-founding- fathers-never-intended-a-permanent-political-class-controlled-by-the-wealthy)

The House of Representatives has averaged 146.7 "legislative days" a year since 2001, according to records kept. ("List of All Sessions." History, Art, & Archives - United States House of Representatives) That's about one day of work every two and a half days.

The Senate, on the other hand, was in session an average of 165 days a year over the same time period. ("Past Days in Session of the U.S. Congress." Congress.gov) They were really slaving away—18 more days.

Have some fun. Do the math:

Using an inflation calculator, the equivalent of a dollar in 1800 (to be approximate) today is $24.14 (as of June 13, 2023). Congressmen were originally only paid $6.00 per day when they were in session. With inflation that means the per day salary equals $144.84.

Remember, the original intent was that congress would only be paid for *the days they were in session.* So, here's the math for our current Congress—

For the House: days in session—146.7 X $144.84 = $21, 248.03

For the Senate: days in session—165 X $144.84 = $23, 898.60

If we base our current Congress's salary on this formula, what are these people going to do to make up the shortfall in their salaries? They might have to return home to engage in some gainful employment. But our elections are not about salaries. Many of these elected officials are not there for the money. They have money. They are there for power and influence. If not, why run campaigns that cost millions and millions of dollars for a position that currently pays $174,000 annually? But we digress...

Yes, we are being a bit facetious with our $6 base. But there's a serious side to this little exercise as well. It says that we might need to make some changes to the way we govern ourselves. And it is for the people to decide not some professional politician or some permanent bureaucrat. They will find it hard to make changes that affect themselves. Unless it is to give themselves a raise.

Change might need to be made because many of those in Congress are acting without regard to the well-being of their constituency. How can we know this? How many homeowners received a bailout when the housing market crashed in 2008? How many banks? Enough said.

The members dutifully accepted the $6 a day salary established when the Constitution was ratified in 1788 and enacted in 1789. At least for a while.

Salary Storm

Angry town hall meetings! Protestors in the street! Attacks by a partisan press! It must be 1816. (Has anything changed?)

Consider having your salary level tied to the market price of wheat. The framers of the Constitution considered that proposal when struggling with the sensitive issue of congressional pay. That $6 for each day per session attended was established in 1789. That was the salary Congress decided to pay senators and representatives.

Before long, senators insisted that they deserved a higher rate of pay than House members. This would reflect senators' stricter constitutional requirements for office, as well as their weighty responsibilities in advising and consenting. The House refused to take that idea seriously—but did agree that someday senators might get $7.

Twenty-seven years later, the cost of living having doubled, members still received $6 a day. This "pitiful sum," complained Kentucky's Richard Mentor Johnson, "might induce a lounging lout to come here," but certainly would not attract a gentleman. He argued that members deserved at least the salary of a good government clerk, which would attract talent and give the poor man a chance to serve. Opponents feared that higher pay would attract scoundrels, not statesmen. South Carolina's Benjamin Huger calculated such a salary to be just "about sufficient to . . . excite the avarice of [a] . . . third-rate county court lawyer."

On March 19, 1816, Congress boldly passed the compensation act, abandoning the $6 per diem in favor of an annual salary of $1500. The result? Outrage!

As the years had passed, members became increasingly dissatisfied with their rates of pay. Hence the March 19, 1816, vote to abandon the $6 daily rate. That rate had amounted to about $900 a year for those who attended regularly. They voted in favor of a $1,500 annual salary. Supporters reasoned that this would make Congress more efficient because members would be less likely to prolong sessions to pile up more daily salary.

It began in the press. Editors charged Congress with "wanton extravagance." Angry public meetings sprang up. Hostile citizens in Georgia hanged their senators in effigy. No one was spared. As New Jersey's Lewis Condit bitterly complained, "I have been dismissed for voting for the bill; one of my colleagues for voting against it; and another one for not voting at all."

Thomas Jefferson, safe in retirement, predicted that "almost the entire mass [of Congress] will go out" with the next election. He was right. A number of senators and two-thirds of the House fell victim to the outrage. Those who survived did so only by promising to repeal the infamous "fifteen-hundred-dollar law."

Why such a violent reaction? Perhaps it was the exceptionally cold weather of 1816 or the lingering economic effects of war with Britain. A combative press certainly fanned the flames of disapproval. As Richard Johnson sadly concluded, the "poor compensation bill excited more discontent than the alien [and] sedition laws, the quasi war with France, the internal taxes of 1798, . . . the late war with Great Britain, the Treaty of Ghent, or any [other] measure of the Government" since 1789.

Frightened "by the angry growls of their constituents," in the words of New Hampshire's Jeremiah Mason, Congress repealed the law. They continued to receive $6 a day. Nearly four decades would pass (not until 1855) before senators and representatives finally received an annual salary. What did they get? $3,000 – roughly equivalent to the salary of a good government clerk.

(Reference Items: From: https://www.senate.gov/about/chronology/1789-1820/senate-salary-1816.htm and U.S. Congress. Senate. The Senate, 1789-1989, Vol. 2, by Robert C. Byrd. 100th Cong., 1st sess., 1991. S. Doc.100-20.)

Our Rest of the Story…
And our point in this bit of history and basic math of Congressional salary structure?

If we do not get the debt under control, the nation will not survive as we know it. A concerted effort is being made by some to destroy the country. They want to "fundamentally change America."

We want to change America fundamentally as well. But the change we are wanting is to return the nation to its founding principles. And the place to begin is getting our debt under control. And the way to begin that is to require our servants to live under the same laws and lifestyles as the average American.

Try that for a while. And change might just come.

Steps to take now:

Action # 1: Contact your representative and senators to urge them to pass a "Balanced Budget Amendment."

Action # 2: Google the national debt clock and watch it for one minute. (https://usdebtclock.org)

Action # 3: Make the national debt a centerpiece of conversation with your representative and hold him/her accountable for wasteful spending.

Action # 4: Take initiative to get out of personal debt including credit cards, car loans, and so forth.

Action # 5: Consider enrolling in a financial seminar provided by your church.

Chapter Six
Considering A New Paradigm

Difficult times demand watchful canary-like citizens. These visionary sentinels consider options that are unconventional to the controlling elites. The financial ills our nation faces do not derive from a single source. Multiple ideologies have been active for over a century and remain intentional in accomplishing their goals in plain view of the public eye.

How is that possible? The average citizen suffers from a general ignorance as to how our economy works. Lack of understanding creates a leadership vacuum allowing the nation to follow a path to economic calamity and disaster if it continues.

Information is power. An informed canary is better prepared to be an influencer on financial decision making. It begins by having a general grasp of economic terminology. Knowing how the peoples' money is manipulated is a critical step to making changes in governmental spending. Here are a few terms to help get you started.

Inflation – is the rate of increase in prices over a given period of time. This includes the overall increases in prices or the increases in the cost of living. It is the erosion of your money's purchasing power.

Stagflation – combines "stagnation" and "inflation." Stagflation is an economic state in which prices keep soaring with economic growth while the rate of increase in the output of goods and services slumps.

Recession – generally, recession is measured at two consecutive quarters of negative gross domestic product (GDP). Another measure is if the GDP (based on the total accumulated production of goods and services in the economy) has declined 1.5 percent in a given year. Economic recessions generally are temporary.

Depression – is recession on steroids. Depression occurs when recession extends over a long period of time. This is a severe decline in the economy lasting for years. The Great Depression lasted from 1929 until the beginning of World War II in 1941.

Hyperinflation – is the result of the price of goods that escalate uncontrollably, leaving consumers unable to afford basic goods. Some of the worst cases of hyperinflation were during the French Revolution when inflation rates hit 143% per month. (Think we have it bad?) But more recent examples are even worse. Included in the list are:

Germany's Weimar Republic (monthly inflation rate of 29,500% in October 1923)

Zimbabwe (monthly inflation rate of 79 billion percent in November 2008—a loaf of bread went from $2 million to $35 million overnight)

Hungary (monthly inflation rate of 13.6 quadrillion percent in 1946)

The reasons for hyperinflation are primarily war and government mis-management of the economy including ill-conceived economic policies like removing any ties of the currency to tangible resources, unrestrained printing of money, generation of large deficits, and price setting. The woes produced by this kind of inflation are unfathomable.

Inflation, stagnation, and recession have been experienced routinely in the lifetime of the most 50-year olds. And do not hear us downplaying the role of inflation. It is pernicious and destructive of most personal budgets across America. During the Jimmy Carter presidency, the inflation rate hit a high of 14.6% in March and April of 1980. It contributed to Carter's defeat in that fall's election. In January 2022, the annual inflation rate was 7.1%, the highest 12-month change since June of 1982. Highest in 40 years. Once inflation gets out of the cage, it is difficult to tame.

Our federal government is printing money like a counterfeit gang. The Inflation Reduction Act (a front for reckless climate change spending sprees) is a prime example of an inflation generator. Inflation occurs when your currency loses its purchasing power. Consumers have more money that buys less. And what's the government's response? Print more money, foolishly believing that flooding the economy with money is the cure for consumer spending and bank lending.

However, if this fresh money supply is not supported by solid economic growth (GDP), businesses will raise their prices to stay in business and consumers will be forced to pay higher prices for goods, services, and interest. Currency inflates while its purchasing power deflates like a balloon with holes.

One conservative senator wrote a constituent who complained to him about the recent debt ceiling debacle. The constituent had written expressing disgust with the outcome.

The senator responded: "Washington's culture of reckless spending is the root cause of our nation's rapidly growing debt burden. Unfortunately, too many in Washington are unwilling to demand fiscal responsibility and a balanced budget.

"I opposed this proposal because it does not make enough progress to rein in D.C.'s fiscal insanity. I believe that any increase in the debt ceiling must be coupled with significant reforms to reduce out-of-control spending. I refuse to stand by and allow Washington's spending addiction to continue putting the security of our nation and our children and grandchildren's futures at risk."

This man gets it! May his tribe increase.

Our federal representatives—who are responsible for the financial house of our nation—should be required to enroll and pass Economics 101. It behooves every American who votes for any member of Congress to understand the nature of economics.

Faithfulness

The word "economics" derives from *oikonomos* and means: steward, overseer, superintendent, or keeper of the house. A steward does not own anything; he or she gladly, meticulously, consistently, and without biases watches over the welfare and wealth of another.

One of the clearest examples of a steward is Joseph, the boy of technicolor-dreamcoat fame. In Genesis, the young dreamer, Joseph was sold into slavery in Egypt. He became the property of a man named Potiphar:

When his master saw that the LORD was with him and made him prosper in all he did, Joseph found favor in his sight and became his personal attendant. Potiphar put him in charge of his household and entrusted him with everything he owned (Gen. 39:4).

Joseph was a steward.

The Apostle Paul stated the one requirement for stewards: *Now it is required of stewards that they be found faithful* (1 Cor. 4:2). Our faithful use of the resources God has given into our care is the basis for our accountability to God.

Jesus always spoke of our relationship to God and the resources He has committed to our oversight as a stewardship. In the teachings of Jesus, God is always the Owner of all. And to the Owner, the steward will give an account. For instance,

- We are to use the resources that God has given us (time, abilities, giftedness, wealth) to help our neighbors (Luke 10: 25-37).

- We are to use the resources committed to us each day with expectation that Jesus could return at any time and demand accountability (Lk. 21:31-48).

104

- Our accountability is proportionate to the resources and responsibilities we have had entrusted to us (Matt. 25:14-30).

And we could go on. Jesus stressed that we are stewards, accountable to God. And faithfulness is the measure of our judgment.

When we think of the issues that can collapse America, the national debt and the debasement of our currency are two of the primary calamities we face. In these, our representatives in the Federal government have been poor stewards. They have enriched themselves. But they have impoverished the rest of us. They have been faithless economists—faithless stewards.

Poor Economists

Economics is the discipline concerned with the production, consumption, and transfer of wealth. Various departments of the federal government are involved in overseeing the economic conditions of our nation. However, the culture of deceit, greed, and control that has evolved in our government demonstrates staggering levels of fiscal incompetence and irresponsibility when it comes to the economy and the general welfare of the citizens of the nation. Today's national leaders are often derelict in performing their oath of office.

Remember, Capitol Hill, from center to circumference, belongs to the people; the elected officials in the Beltway have been sent by the people and should remain there as long as they demonstrate the servant attitudes of a steward. Sadly, it appears too many of these professional politicians have not been taught how to manage the peoples' money. Or they choose blatantly to continue reckless spending patterns.

It's time to consider other paradigms. Thinking people know the mess our nation is facing because of fiscal incompetence demonstrated for decades. It's been 2000 years since Jesus revealed a paradigm shift for His listeners. All three Synoptic gospel writers (Matthew, Mark, Luke) record these living words that are pertinent for today—

No one puts a piece of unshrunk cloth on an old garment, for the patch tears away from the garment and a worse tear is made. Neither is new wine put in old wineskins. If it is, the skins burst and the wine is spilled and the skins are destroyed. But new wine is put into fresh wineskins, and so both are preserved.

Matthew 9:14-17; Mark 2:18-22; Luke 5:33-39

Two specific areas that should raise a collective eyebrow of Christian canaries across this culture are—
1. Calling the bluff on debt ceiling dialogue.
2. Calling attention to the Deep State connection with the Federal Reserve System.

The need for *new wine skins* is obvious. What might a paradigm shift look like when these two issues are addressed by intentional canaries?

A Novel Idea

What would happen if the American people called the bluff on debt ceiling discussions? What if the deadline for raising the debt limit were to come and go?

Let that happen. Here's a scenario to consider. Suppose our federal government called up debtors and said, "Sorry, but we are going to have to stop paying our debts to you."

Default is always held over the public's head like Poe's Pendulum—"We must pay our bills. We must pay our debts. The full faith and credit of the United States are at stake." And we dutifully raise the debt ceiling and print more fiat currency. In the process of the regressive tax of inflation, we rob the working Americans of comfort, hopes, and dreams.

We have enough cash flow to pay our requirements, including the interest on our loans. We could call a halt long enough to figure out how to stop the madness. But the slaves to the system (our politicians) keep right on with business as usual. They get rich doing it. It might not be out-and-out bribes. But how many cushy, no-show jobs await them when they leave office?

Meanwhile the citizens get poorer and our country is pushed closer to the brink of the financial abyss.

What if the federal government had to declare the obvious—bankruptcy?

Bankruptcy protection is designed to help financially challenged people establish a court-ordered and directed plan to repay their debts. America is bankrupt now. We are the world's largest debtor nation. We are so broke, we can't pay attention. We are so broke, we don't even have two cents to put into the conversation. We have been such poor stewards of our status and resources that a significant collection of the world's nations is in process of developing a competing currency to the U.S. dollar.

Our greatest export since the end of World War II has been the United States' dollar. It has been the world's reserve currency, replacing the British pound. Our worst exports have been our inflation and our debt. The world of the developing economies led by the BRICS nations are telling us that they are through with the dollar. It might take some time. Replacement is unlikely in the short-term. However, we need to be listening to the signals that are being sent. It will be a competing currency. We are not invincible. We will feel some pain out of this move, if they can gain cooperation between themselves.

It is time to stop throwing good money after bad money. Maybe a federal spending plan, called a "budget" is directed by the Supreme Court. Is it possible that government waste could be discovered and removed? Politicians are always talking about it. Stop talking and do something about it.

Bankruptcy would be painfully difficult to manage. Stock prices could plummet say the pundits. A positive element to this suggestion is that our generation takes seriously the financially mess that we refuse to pass on to the next generation of taxpayers. And the world might actually respect the move.

It seems to be an insane proposal, but no more moronic than current attitudes toward spending in Washington D. C. It's time to stand up against this bully.

And speaking of bullies—
What if we said to China, "Your biological weapon, COVID-19, killed more than 1 million of our citizens and cost our nation trillions of dollars. Moving forward, our position will be that our outstanding loans to your nation are considered paid in full."

China created some of our debt problem. The virus appears to have been intentionally released on the world by China. Look at the economic devastation not to mention the pain and suffering, the loss of life, the loss of freedom—globally. Let them feel some heavy financial pain.

Just a thought.

Debasement
Empires rise and fall. The Roman Empire almost collapsed hundreds of years before it actually fell. The near-collapse came in the period from A.D. 235-284. It is known as the Crisis of the Third Century. The near collapse was caused by a number of factors:

1. The problem of succession and civil war (Fragmentation)
2. Natural disasters (a plague/pandemic, a mega-drought in western Asia) with an open border allowed the Germanic tribes from the north to invade
3. *Debasement of the Currency and Hyperinflation*
4. Breakdown of internal trade networks
5. Widespread civil unrest
6. Falling revenues and increasing expenses of the Empire
7. Increased militarization

Sound familiar? Let's just substitute the United States for the Roman Empire in this scenario. Change the northern border for our southern border. Look at how many ways we are fragmented as a society. Wide spread civil unrest—can we recall the "summer of love" with its riots across America in 2020?

A failing economy was one of the primary causes of the near-collapse. Driven by the debasement of the currency and hyperinflation, life for the average Roman citizen became harsh and unbearable.

For the average American citizen today, we are feeling some sympathy for the Romans of the Third Century. Our currency has been debased and our dollars cannot cover the expenses of our lives. It was not always this way.

Various inflation calculators are available online. We found one that allowed us to look at the inflation rate from the inception of the settlements in America from 1635-Present (https://www.in2013dollars.com/). If you have a strong stomach, you can have some fun with this. It is eye-opening.

We wanted to know about two timeframes: 1800-1913 and 1913-2023. Here's what we discovered using the value of $1.00—

1800-1913

A dollar in 1800 was equivalent in purchasing power to about $0.79 in 1913, a difference of $-0.21 over 113 years. The dollar had an average deflation rate of -0.21% per year since 1800, producing a cumulative price change of -21.43%.

This means that prices in 1913 were 21.43% *lower* than average prices since 1800 according to the Bureau of Labor Statistics consumer price index. Your dollar would have MORE purchasing power in 1913 than in 1800.

1913-2023

A dollar in 1913 was equivalent in purchasing power to about $30.72 today, an increase of $29.72 over 110 years. The dollar had an average inflation rate of 3.16% per year between 1913 and today, producing a cumulative price increase of 2,971.99%.

This means that today's prices are 30.72 times as high as average prices since 1913 according to the Bureau of Labor Statistics consumer price index. A dollar today only buys 3.255% of what it could buy back then. We don't really have to spell that out, do we? You work harder and longer for dollars that have been reduced to near-zero in purchasing power.

If a dozen eggs cost $1.00 in 1913, you couldn't even buy one egg with one of today's dollars. Been to the grocery store lately?

The Personal Story

Inflation is a loss of purchasing power. The talking heads in media and even economists talk of inflation as "too much money chasing too few goods." That is meaningless to the average person. Inflation is the debasement and dilution of the currency.

Let's translate this into a specific, personal experience. An older friend was listening to all the talk about inflation and experiencing it personally every time he went to the grocery or fuel pump. He came across an inflation calculator online. He decided to figure out how inflation had affected him.

Here's something that was a concrete, personal experience. My friend graduated with a Masters degree in 1975. His first job paid $12,000. So he plugged into the inflation calculator the date of 1975 and the calculator displayed that the current amount required to equal the earning power of a 1975 dollar was $5.61 in today's dollars. To equal the same purchasing power as his 1975 salary, my friend had to earn $67,320.

The kicker in this little exercise—my friend, in his last year of work, earned $70,000. That's a nice salary. But the sad part for my friend was that at the end of his career, his annual purchasing power had only increased by $2,680. And put that over a 50-year career. It meant that the increase in his true purchasing power had averaged only $53.60 per year.

That's how inflation works. It is the debasement of the currency. More dollars are required to buy less. A lot less.

Like with Paul Harvey's great line, "And now for the rest of the story—."

My friend was a minister. Spent 50 years in ministry. His last salary was basically equal to his first salary out of seminary. Had God not blessed? Yes, He had. Ask my friend if he has led a blessed life and he will with full-voice tell you he had a blessed life. Did his paycheck reflect that? No. But the investment he made in people, in the Kingdom of God, enriched his life beyond measure.

Would he have liked a bit more money? Maybe. Could he have used it rearing his children, doing his ministry? Undoubtedly. In the words of Joe Louis, heavy-weight boxing champion, "Money don't make me happy. But it sure does calm my nerves."

For this man of God, it was not about money. It was about mission. He never went to a new position for more money. Every move was measured in the light of opportunity and God's will.

But there is a sadness to this story, not for this man. It is for our nation. A nation who has been sold out by bankers and politicians. A nation whose currency, labor, and creativity have been debased. It's time for the people who are in charge of this nation to rise up and say, "Enough!"

How have we come to this point?

Deception

G. Edward Griffin, author of *The Creature from Jekyll Island*, related this account of the beginning of the Federal Reserve—

"In 1910, six wealthy New York bankers traveled to a private club on a private island off the Georgia coast—Jekyll Island. They had agreed to travel with as little attention to themselves as possible. They arrived separately at the train station. Some traveled under assumed names. If they encountered one another on the train, they pretended not to know one another. Under the pretention of a duck hunting trip, these men gathered. One didn't even own a shotgun. He had to borrow one. Their travel was just the beginning their deception. It would never change.

"Over a few days, these bankers formed a cartel that would operate under the identity of the Federal Reserve System—a central bank like those of Europe. And an idea that was rejected by the founders and the early leaders of the new nation." (For more information than we have space and need to delve into, consider looking at the following: https://www.federalreservehistory.org/essays/jekyll-island-conference; *The Creature from Jekyll Island* by G. Edward Griffin)

One of the tasks to deceive the nation was in the design of the very name. They decided to call it the *Federal Reserve System*. A lie in itself. It is not *Federal*—it is a private banking cartel. It is not a *Reserve*—it creates money out of thin air. It has no reserves. They called it a *System*—only to give the appearance that it is regional in its nature. It scattered branches over the United States but they operate under one central structure.

Acting in concert with their overlords, the Congress passed the Federal Reserve Act of 1913. The stated goals for this entity are to maintain and assure:

- maximum employment
- stable prices
- moderate long-term interest rates

How's that working out for you?

Let's just take one snapshot to see how effective the Federal Reserve is at doing their publicly stated job. The following chart covers the years since 1950. Every one of these peaks represents a recession. (Don't try to read that small print—the peaks represent the unemployment rate.) The chart provides a general impression, a pattern for how well the Fed is fulfilling their mandates.

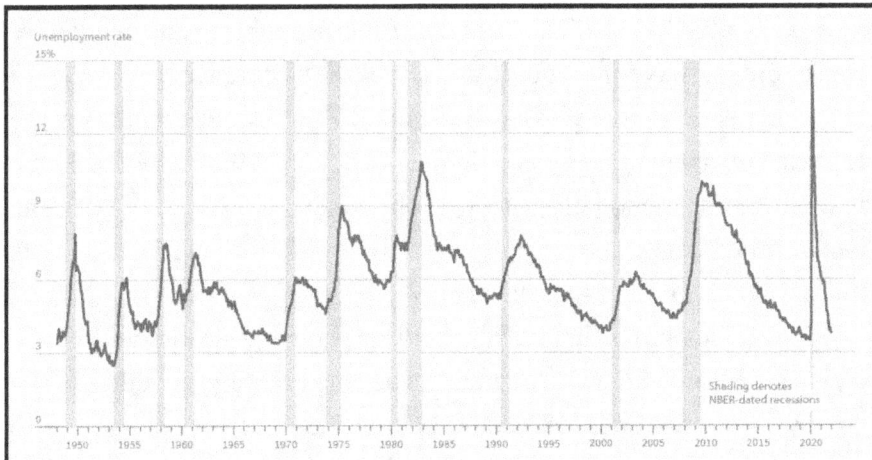

Remember that interest rate stability mandate? Stable for whom? You? Who are the only ones making money this whole time? Who are the ones getting bailed out? We are not getting bailed out. We are getting thrown under the bus.

Currently, three banks have failed in 2023. Silicon Valley Bank, First Republic Bank, and Signature Bank have collapsed costing taxpayers millions of dollars to guarantee winners and losers. The winners are stock-holders; the losers are depositors or well-contributing clients who are protected up to $250,000 through the Federal Deposit Insurance Cap (FDIC).

How did these banks fail? Follow the money. Banks borrow money from the Federal Reserve who charges interest on those funds. The bank then loans these monies to the public at a higher rate of interest. The difference is profit. So, here is what happened with these failures.

Let's suppose that Bank A borrowed funds at a two percent interest rate. They loan the monies at prime plus a certain percentage. When the federal government foolishly flooded the economy with wasteful spending called, "The Inflation Reduction Act," the result was inflation that reached levels not felt in 40 years. Sky-rocketing inflation means higher interest rates demanded by the Federal Reserve to the banks who loaned money at much lower rates. That means, banks like Silicon Valley, First Republic, and Signature Banks did not have the liquidity to cover the difference.

Such short sightedness was a bust for banks but a boon for the federal government. How? Before the bank failures of 2023, the federal government held one trillion dollars in assets. After the banks failed, these assets ballooned to seven trillion dollars. Was this a planned, forced foreclosure?

The elites have figured out how to privatize profits and publicize debt. Remember the mantra, "The full faith and credit..." The taxpayers are the ones who stand behind the debt. We all go out to dinner—the elites, the bankers from the Federal Reserve, the politicians, and the average citizen. The elites, the bankers behind the Federal Reserve, and the pols get the most expensive entrées on the menu and we, the average citizen, get the tab. They don't even pick up the tip!

Look at the chart on page 80 again. That's the debt you and I owe. Can we expect to owe more or less by this time next year?

One wit said: "We don't need to audit the Fed. We need to abolish it." He's right.

One person asked, "How would that work?" A return to original design is the answer. The House of Representatives would appropriate the money. The Treasury, under the authority of the President, would be responsible for managing the money coming into and being distributed by the federal government. If the Treasury did what they were designed to do, we would not need the Federal Reserve. If expanded responsibilities were required of the Treasury, they could be added to reflect the evolving economic and technological environment.

Who's in Charge?

When we ask this question, we are not speaking just of those who sit in the houses of Congress or reside temporarily in the White House. We speak of those President Abraham Lincoln had in mind when he made some brief remarks at the dedication of a battlefield cemetery. He was asked to make a few remarks at the close of the ceremonies. His words have become one of the more profound statements about the nature of our nation in its entire history. Take just a moment to rehearse the words we looked at earlier—

"It is for us the living, rather, to be dedicated here to the unfinished work which they who fought here have thus far so nobly advanced. It is rather for us to be here dedicated to the great task remaining before us—that from these honored dead we take increased devotion to that cause for which they here gave the last full measure of devotion—that we here highly resolve that these dead shall not have died in vain—that this nation, under God, shall have a new birth of freedom, and that government of the people, by the people, for the people, shall not perish from the earth."

Gettysburg, Pennsylvania
19th November, 1863

This government of the United States was not designed as overlords. It is not a feudal system. (Although it is rapidly becoming one.) It is a government **of, by**, and **for** the people. Us. The citizens.

Because the Congress and the President are elected by the citizens, we the people are ultimately in charge. It is time for the people who own this government to arise and demand accountability from our employees, that is our government—elected and unelected. Fiscal responsibility is one of the first places to begin.

Wake up! Fiscally responsible canaries are needed in this economic coal mine like never before. How many of us will finally step up to declare, "It's time to stop the insanity!"

Steps to take now:

Action # 1: Learn the terminology of Economics and discover how the consequences connected to these terms used in this chapter affect your lifestyle.

Action # 2: Set a savings goal. Six months of income is a great start.

Action # 3: Consult Americafirstpolicyinstitute.com to discover how our nation can unleash American prosperity and ingenuity.

Action # 4: Contact your congressional representative with a call for action concerning unleashing our energy abundance so we as a nation will become energy independent.

Chapter Seven
The Accountability Factor

Accountability is not a new concept in our way of life. Like spokes in a wheel, we all have several different strands of accountability. We are accountable to people and organizations. Holding a job means submitting to someone in authority. An employer has every right to challenge job performance. Married people have expectations that hold each other accountable.

Just like most of us are accountable in some form or fashion, our elected leaders, our representatives are to be held accountable to those people they were elected to serve. Every politician whether local, state, or federal is accountable to taxpayers. These representatives are not overlords. They are stand-ins for us.

A baseball batter's box illustrates accountability. During the initial innings of a game, the lines for that box are clear. However, as the game progresses, these lines of demarcation become muddled. Savvy batters can intentionally step beyond these lines to gain an advantage on the pitcher. Our federal government has made muddling accountability lines an art form, especially when it comes to applying justice equally.

Our culture should be grateful to be Americans. You might recall the days when elementary school began with each class standing to attention, facing the Stars and Stripes, placing hands over hearts, and then reciting *The Pledge of Allegiance.* These inspiring words were penned by Francis Bellamy on September 8, 1892, with the purpose of teaching generations (not indoctrinate as some espouse) the importance of being loyal to our nation and to a way of life.

"I pledge allegiance to the Flag of the United States of America, and to the Republic for which it stands, one Nation under God, indivisible, with liberty and justice for all."

Read that last phrase again...*liberty and justice for all.* Justice! For all! Not for a few nor for a select self-aggrandizing group of aristocrats. Whether rich or poor, black or white, male or female, and regardless of political persuasion, justice has been woven into the very fabric of our historic culture. Every citizen, regardless of race, creed, financial or social status, is to have access to it. The Fourteenth Amendment assures justice for all Americans. It reads,

> *"No State shall make or enforce any law which shall abridge the privileges or immunities of citizens of the United States; nor shall any State deprive any person of life, liberty, or property, without due process of law; nor deny to any person within its jurisdiction the equal protection of the laws."*

Because those framers of the Constitution were conscious of the presence of Almighty God and grounded in biblical authority, they wrote with a biblical understanding of justice. The Holy Scriptures are replete with the call for equity in justice and warnings against injustice.

Justice in the Old Testament

The Old Testament provides multiple examples of how justice is to be applied. Because they were burdened over the moral decay of their beloved nation, the prophets were commissioned to address justice and to stand against injustice.

A bit of clarification is necessary—prophets were "forth-tellers." These were people through whom God spoke. They would proclaim, *Thus saith the Lord....* They were not looking into crystal balls and seeing upcoming events. They simply spoke the message that God was giving them. They were listening to the voice of God. God was the one seeing the future. God's essential attributes include omniscience, omnipresence, omnipotence. He is everywhere present. He transcends time and space. He knows the end from the beginning.

Because of His transcendence, when God judges a person, a nation, or an action, His pronouncements and judgements are just. Because He is just, He demands justice in our thoughts and our actions.

The prophets spoke as they were moved by the Spirit of God: *For no prophecy was ever produced by the will of man, but men spoke from God as they were carried along by the Holy Spirit* (1 Peter 1:21). The writer of Hebrews opened his letter by stating that God had spoken in days past to the fathers of their nation by the prophets: *Long ago, at many times and in many ways, God spoke to our fathers by the prophets* (Hebrews 1:1). And as we read these prophets, we hear the voice of God calling for accountability.

Three of these biblical canaries come to mind: Amos, Micah, and Isaiah. Though speaking to generations thousands of years ago, their words ring with truth for a culture in free fall.

Consider the life, times, and message of Amos who spoke out during the middle of the 8th century B.C. Prosperity and national security reigned in the Northern Kingdom as well as the Southern Kingdom. Peace was apparent in every sector of that ancient culture. However, Israel had turned their backs on the Lord and their worship had become perfunctory and empty. The Northern Kingdom became saturated with immorality and idolatry. Injustice became commonplace. Amos highlighted the injustice noting how the rich trampled the rights of the poor. Amos' prophecy is about justice, especially social justice. This ancient canary fearlessly said,

"But let justice roll down like waters and righteousness like an ever-flowing stream."

119

In time, God acted to execute justice because His essential nature is just. As the absolute Creator of everything, according to Amos 4:13, 5:8; 9:5-6, the Lord remains in authority even if a nation (past or present) refuses to acknowledge that authority. Clearly, the Lord rejects the moral and ethical practices inherent in injustice.

Sadly, a nation that practices indiscriminate injustice does not realize a day of accounting is coming.

Micah was another ancient canary whose message clearly announced the Lord's patience and long-suffering. However, because the Lord is just, He would not tolerate the actions of Judah and Israel's corrupt leaders. The Lord was not going to wink at their greed, oppression, and exploitation of the poor (Micah 1:3, 4, 6, 7; 3:5, 11; 4:9-12; 6:10, 11, 16; 7:5- 6).

The central message of Micah is simply stated: *"Do justice, love kindness and walk humbly with God."*

The message of these two prophets is echoed by Isaiah. He lamented that justice was not to be found in any sector of his culture. Because he witnessed the last years of the spiritual decline of Israel, his passionate words to Judah are sharp and spoken with urgency.

Isaiah 59 is an unmistakable and divine view toward justice. Future canaries can learn from their ancestors by applying insights from these images.

Image # 1 – Wash your hands! (1-3)

We tie God's hands from working because our hands are defiled. Dirty hands signal the presence of dirty hearts. And defiled hearts spew vile thoughts that lead to twisted views of justice.

Image # 2 – Watch that poison! (4-5)

Lying is at the root of all injustice. It's not just words spoken into the air or written on a piece of paper. A lie will develop a life of its own. Today's justice system resembles a metastasizing cancer that is poisoning our culture because some use empty pleas to speak lies that conceive mischief. From mischief is born injustice.

Image # 3 – Wear proper clothing! (6-8)

Sir Walter Scott once declared, "O, what a tangled web we weave when first we practice to deceive!" Injustice is riddled with deception. Like Scott, Isaiah points to the folly of dressing in a spider's web. It's impossible to hide anything behind a spider's web—including lying injustice.

Image # 4 – Weep for authority! (9-13)

Like a traffic jam on a city highway at rush hour, their ancient culture was stuck with no place to turn. Truth had been trampled in the streets and progress had stopped. The divine authorities of "justice and righteousness" stood far away from the mayhem because the people refused authority. Sound familiar? This ancient scene resembles our culture today, doesn't it?

Image # 5 – Wait for leadership! (16-21)

The eyes of the Lord search for canaries who will intercede for their culture. He found none in Isaiah's culture. Were He to look in your city, street, home, church, would He find a caring canary who would faithfully sound the alarm against injustices?

The anthem for justice should be Isaiah's words:
Woe to those who call evil good and good evil,
who put darkness for light and light for darkness,
who put bitter for sweet and sweet for bitter!
Woe to those who are wise in their own eyes,
and shrewd in their own sight!
Woe to those who are heroes at drinking wine,
and valiant men in mixing strong drink,
who acquit the guilty for a bribe,

and deprive the innocent of his right!
Therefore, as the tongue of fire devours the stubble,
and as dry grass sinks down in the flame, so their root will be as
rottenness, and their blossom go up like dust;
for they have rejected the law of the Lord of hosts,
and have despised the word of the Holy One of Israel.
Therefore the anger of the Lord was kindled against his people,
and he stretched out his hand against them and struck them,
and the mountains quaked; and their corpses were as refuse
in the midst of the streets.
For all this his anger has not turned away,
and his hand is stretched out still (Isaiah 5:20-25).

Hundreds of years passed before another advocate for justice arrived in Judah's culture. His words are recorded in Matthew 23:23-24. Speaking to lawyers of His day, Jesus warned,

*"**Woe** to you, scribes and Pharisees, hypocrites! For you tithe mint and dill and cumin and have neglected the weightier matters of the law: **justice and mercy and faithfulness**. These you ought to have done, without neglecting others. You blind guides, straining out a gnat and swallowing a camel."*

Jesus reflected the same demands found in the prophets of Amos, Micah, and Isaiah. Why? Because God's standard has never changed. The attribute God has revealed is immutability. That means that the nature, character, and conduct of God has not and will not change. As He called through Micah for justice, mercy, and humble, faithful relationship, God did the same through His Son. God's standard for justice stands for America today.

Too big to fail; too big to jail.
The parallels between our times and that of ancient Judah are astounding. A culture in free fall seems to struggle with misapplica-

122

tion of laws and prejudices when laws are applied. Today our broken legal system smacks of hypocrisy at the highest levels of our federal government. When it comes to injustice in our culture, it is feared that our nation's leaders are picking winners and losers. Due process afforded by the 14th Amendment is routinely ignored.

Lady Justice wears a blindfold and firmly holds a set of scales for a reason. A symbol of the legal system, her image is based on the Greek goddess Themis and the Roman goddess Justitia. Both were known for their good judgment and righteousness. It's a reminder that the courts of our land exist to protect the rights of the people without being influenced by outside factors. Thus, the phrase, "justice is blind" was born.

Our culture cries for canaries to protect us from a corrupt legal system. Heavy-handed bureaucrats continually tip the scales of justice. Amos called out the injustice of those who literally were tipping the scales:

Hear this, you who trample on the needy and bring the poor of the land to an end, saying, "When will the new moon be over, that we may sell grain? And the Sabbath, that we may offer wheat for sale, that we may make the ephah small and the shekel great and deal deceitfully with false balances, that we may buy the poor for silver and the needy for a pair of sandals and sell the chaff of the wheat (Amos 8:4-6)?"

The rich were dealing unjustly with the poor. They were selling smaller amounts for greater prices. They put their thumbs on the scales, cheating those who could least afford it.

God announced that justice was coming. He showed Amos a plumb line (7:8-9), a standard of measurement. A plumb line is a definitive means of measuring a line that is perfectly straight up and down with gravity. Through the use of this image, God is saying that the standard of His justice will be the measure against which judgment will be delivered.

Injustice often remains in the dark for years. Until it is revealed, injustice will race through a culture like a prairie fire. God will bring the perfect measure of justice to individuals and to nations. Amos proclaimed that judgment was coming to Israel, the Northern Kingdom. It came in the form of the Assyrian Empire. This long-lived empire served as God's instrument of retribution.

The practice of the Assyrians, as mentioned earlier, was to disperse captive people into their general population. They mixed them so thoroughly that they were absorbed into the population mix of the Assyrian Empire. Those people lost their identity. That is exactly what happened to the Northern kingdom of Israel. So complete was the dispersion that the ten tribes composing the Northern Kingdom have forever been known as the ten lost tribes of Israel.

When God brings judgment, it is complete and just.

Justice Is Demanded in America

The brilliant light of justice needs to shine again. The kind of light that illuminates corruption that systemically practices injustice. How many illustrations does one need that show bureaucratic dishonesty and favoritism? What emotions are invoked when you hear names like: Hillary Clinton, Eric Holder, Lois Lerner, Hunter Biden, Merrick Garland, or Christopher Wray? Do you feel that accountability and honesty have been practiced? Has equality before the Law been evidenced? Have the scales of Blind Justice remained unweighted and unbiased?

What feelings are generated when you think of Antifa or Black Lives Matter? What about injustices on display in America's courtrooms? Increasingly, if radicals cannot get what they want at the ballot box, they turn to violence in the streets and injustice in the courtrooms. Lawfare is becoming the primary means of domination and control for far leftists.

Funded by the public coffers, leftist groups, District Attorneys, Attorneys General, and judges are waging war in the courtrooms. Draining the resources of accused and indicted citizens is part of the game. Smearing reputations, restricting speech, disqualification—lawfare is becoming the primary strategy for power and control.

Injustice! We need not search for obscure instances. Examples scream from headlines, news outlets, podcasts. During the Soviet era, show trials were held as an example and warning of what could happen to others if the State so desired. A show trial was a public trial in which the guilt or innocence of a defendant had already been determined. These trials were aimed at specific groups or individuals the State designated as enemies and used for propaganda purposes. The message became clear—comply or you could be next.

The lawfare being conducted in courtrooms across America today are taking on the same purposes.

Just ask Daniel Penny. Penny invested four years in the Marines, rising to the rank of sergeant. He received numerous awards including the Marine Corps Good Conduct Medal. However, this patriot was indicted for manslaughter and released on a $100,000 bail. What was his crime?

The presence of crime is a well-known reality by New Yorkers who utilize the subways. On May 1, 2023 while riding in Gotham's subway system, Penny and two other men (who remain unnamed) were forced to subdue a deranged individual who was threatening passengers on the F train. Penny is a magnificent example of a canary in a coal mine. His reward? The Manhattan District Attorney moved this case into the fast lane by avoiding a Grand Jury indictment of Penny without due process of the law.

Such lawfare being inflicted on individuals or groups across the country is destructive. Such a perverted process rots the soul of our culture when citizens face injustice at the hands of the ruling factions. You want to find where injustice is reigning? Look no further than New York, Chicago, Los Angles, Seattle, Portland, Denver, St. Louis and any of a number of cities and states where leftists are in power. The scales of justice do not just have a thumb on them. They have been ripped from the hand of Lady Justice.

Injustice! Justice delayed is justice denied. How many citizens are sitting in squalid conditions in jails being denied a day in court? Where is the right to a speedy trial by a jury of one's peers?

Injustice! It appears some in our culture too big to fail, too big to jail. Additional examples of injustices in our culture include:

"A Summer of Love"

More than 50 years have passed since our nation experienced a social phenomenon called, "the Summer of Love." That was when more than 100,000 young people who were tagged "hippies," converged in San Francisco's neighborhood of Haight-Ashbury. This eclectic group was known for their fashion of dress, music, hallucinogenic drugs, anti-war views, and free love.

Turn back the page to the year 2020 where riots which some biased reporters called, "a summer of love" were lead stories of national news agencies for months. Cries of injustice were heard across the nation. Amazing how our federal government routinely winks at hundreds of crimes at the cost of billions of dollars.

Injustice occurs when our government turns a deaf ear and a blind eye to crimes that do not fit their political narrative. Yet, seeks to make examples of innocent pedestrians who happened to tread the Capitol grounds on January 6, 2021. Show trials, anyone?

Injustice on the Border

Legal immigration is what made our country great. America is the melting pot of the world and the envy of people living under oppression and subjugation around the globe. These "dreamers" hear of America's greatness and then begin the process of immigration into our country. The legal process for becoming a self-sufficient American citizen takes years and allows assimilation into the culture.

However, that scenario has been systematically dismantled by federal administration officials. Nations are identified by demarked borders. No borders; no nation. Yet, the southern border of our country especially has been invaded by more than six million illegal aliens in the last three years. Some of these people are—

Criminals – Unlawful entry is a felony offense.

Drug Dealers – Recently, the DEA seized more than 50 million fentanyl pills and more than 10,500 pounds of fentanyl powder. This represents more than 379 million potential deadly doses of this dangerous drug. That's enough to kill every American. (By the way, our Chinese enemies are the suppliers of the raw ingredients for fentanyl.)

Sexual Exploiters – Mexican cartels charge thousands of dollars for illegal women to be led across our border. These women pay back this "loan" by becoming prostitutes. And what is worse is the trafficking of children. The innocents have their lives destroyed. And who is one of the top markets? America. If God does not bring judgment upon our nation, He owes apologies to Sodom and Gomorrah.

A Public Burden – Economic refugees stream by millions to America. But economics are not the basis for asylum. These illegals flooding across the border are provided shelter, food, clothing, cell phones, transportation, education, medical coverage, and legal representation—all for free. At least to them. The bill comes to us, the American taxpayers.

Free? Nothing is free. These illegals are crossing the border to live on our dimes. We pay for it through the wasteful spending of the federal government. What are our government officials thinking? It depends on which aisle is persuading our culture.

It is apparent that Democrats welcome illegals because they want a dependent class who will be future voters. How? When a baby is born on American soil, that child is an American citizen. And an anchor for the entire family seeking entry into America. Imagine what our country will look like as these "dependent" people enter polling booths across the nation.

Republicans might be no different. They are not necessarily looking for votes. They welcome cheap labor. Drive by any large cash crop and you will likely see these impoverished souls in the fields. Have you noticed who is building our houses, mowing our yards, and performing every kind of menial labor possible?

America has a generous immigration policy. However, it is a legal process. Illegal incursion—breaking line—breaks the system and weakens the nation. It makes a mockery of the notion of a sovereign nation. If we have no borders, no common language, no common culture, eventually, we will have no nation.

Injustice uses people and loves things; justice loves people and uses things. Our broken immigration system is injustice for all.

Conditioned and Desensitized

Should we be aware of social conditioning from multiple directions? Every canary must answer that for himself and herself. A review of social conditioning by the federal government is alarming. And while we cannot address all of the issues in detail, here are a few examples of how we have been conditioned and desensitized.

We have moved from justice to operating a "legal system."

The legal profession is a finely oiled machine. The average American has difficulty receiving justice in courts due in part to the expense of it. One strategy of many corporate attorneys is to force a defendant into lower settlements. If that settlement is not agreed between two parties, the corporate attorneys begin the process of a financial slow bleed of defendants. This is a form of lawfare. Too often, an "injured" defendant realizes the legal process is not sustainable financially. Also, attorneys utilize "delay" tactics that prove to be expensive for common people seeking justice.

Currently 63% of our federal legislators are attorneys. They have learned how to litigate but do not know how to lead. That's why we have stalemates in Congress. The influence of statesmen or stateswomen seem benign in those Capitol Hill chambers. They are present but they are not leading as needed.

We are being conditioned through social media.

After the attacks on September 11, 2001, the federal government launched a plan to identify terrorists by linking with technology. Along the way, Facebook was/is utilized to introduce "facial recognition." Selfies of people and their relationships saturated this technology. Big Brother is watching again! It's a way to gain control of the people. Social media platforms have been utilized to control the messages people are able to receive and evaluate.

The Fourth Branch of the Federal Government.

Lobbyists. These organizations exist to influence our elected officials by applying continual pressure to conform to their demands. They are key in shaping an avalanche of Congregational legislation.

For example, "The Inflation Reduction Act" was a ruse for spending tax dollars on green energy. It did not reduce inflation. Inflation exploded costing typical families and causing them to make tough economic choices. General food staples, gas, and the price of every item under the sun were affected by lobbying influences. Lobbying influencers assist their clients unlock huge sums of governmental funding that has been authorized by a bipartisan infrastructure law and navigate a multitude of regulatory proposals.

Like termites, multitudes of lobbyists exist to operate behind the scenes and beyond searching eyes. All the while destroying the infrastructure that keeps our nation's house standing.

The fallacy of the Fauci fiasco.

Anthony Fauci, former Chief Medical Advisor to the President, was in the right place at the wrong time. Hindsight is 20/20. The conditioning that occurred during Covid-19 pandemic aptly illustrates a carefully crafted plan to control Americans. Covid became an excuse for the federal government to seize control of the entire nation.

Fear and intimidation were two effective tools used against us.

Do you recall Covid restrictions such as wearing masks and then more masks, getting shots and booster shots and being ostracized from certain businesses and restaurants until immunization certificates were presented? Masks are like stopping a mosquito from traveling through a chain link fence.

Did you feel uncomfortable when walking down a grocery store isle that had footprints pointing the opposite direction? What about keeping 6 feet away from others? Did you ever have to stand outside a business to wait for people to go out the back door so you could enter the front door? Remember the clicker/counter? You couldn't go into some stores until another person left. And we all followed along like sheep to the slaughter.

Essential businesses thrived. Wal-Mart, Home Depot, golf courses, and even liquor stores were considered, "essential businesses." Amazingly, the church was not allowed to congregate under pressure from the federal government. There goes the first amendment.

"Shelter in place" was the phrase used to keep order in the culture by our elected officials. The "do-as-I-say-not-as-I-do" politicians oftentimes were exposed by their lack of compliance. Like the former Speaker of the House, Nancy Pelosi, getting her hair done. Going out to dinner or having fund-raisers for wealthy donors where the guests were unmasked but the serving staff were all masked up.

The farce of Fauci is considered by some to be a "test" of the gullibility levels by Americans. And the conditioning that occurred is preparing us for the next phase of control.

The Absence of Leadership

For our culture to thrive again, leaders will be required to step up in a quartet of arenas. Four specific areas are affected by the absence of leadership.

1. The family – the absence of fathers.

The number of homes without fathers present has left a path of destruction through our culture more devastating than any hurricane imaginable. And the trend of fatherless homes has increased in recent decades. The impact a father has on his children's lives cannot be overstated. When a father leaves his family—whether physically or emotionally—the effect on his kids can be damaging.

Children who grow up without a father's presence and involvement are more likely to:

- have behavioral problems
- drop out of school
- face depression, anxiety, or other mental health issues
- struggle financially
- become sexually promiscuous and/or face teenage pregnancy
- use drugs and alcohol
- become aggressive or violent
- leave their own children when they become parents

Dr. Bob Woodson has written insightfully about the dissolution of the black family. He has asserted that until the mid-60s when the War on Poverty was launched, 85% of all black families had two parents rearing their children. Since the advent of the Welfare State and the War on Poverty, more than 75% of black children are born to single mothers.

The welfare system that was instituted included penalties for marriage and work. Benefits would be decreased or terminated. When income was detached from work, the role of fathers in the family was diminished, if not destroyed. The destruction of the black family was considered acceptable collateral damage in this new war. Some suggest that the black family was a primary target.

The war was driven by a strategy developed by Columbia University professors Richard Cloward and Frances Fox Piven. This "Cloward and Piven Strategy" promoted a massive rise of dependency within the welfare system. The goal was to overload the U.S.

public welfare system to the point of collapsing it. When the system collapsed, a new radical system could be instituted. Two terms under Obama and now with a third led by his henchmen and women surrounding the declining occupant in the White House, the country is on the verge of destruction.

Black Lives Matter Global Network Foundation was founded in 2013 by three women who claimed themselves Marxists. This group is often identified as the voice of the larger social movement Black Lives Matter. But it is not. It is a private organization just riding the wave of contributions and publicity for the moment.

The group raised concerns when the public began seeing on the foundation's web site their list of stated beliefs. One statement in particular alarmed people the most:

"We disrupt the Western-prescribed nuclear family structure requirement by supporting each other as extended families and villages that collectively care for one another, especially our children, to the degree that mothers, parents, and children are comfortable."

Now there is clarity in the phrase, "It takes a village to raise a child." The object of Marxists is to decrease parental authority. And to transfer that authority for the child to a culture in free fall.

The statement from Black Lives Matter Global Network Foundation alarmed conservatives and libertarians. The group's beliefs, practices, and management came under greater scrutiny. This statement was removed from the foundation's website in 2020. But just removing the statement from a web site does not remove it from the group's agenda. When they tell you their objectives, believe them.

How cynical can a group of people be to want to destroy families and lives to create conditions for their radical, Marxist agenda!

Leading Voices

Dr. Walter E. Williams and Dr. Thomas Sowell have addressed the destruction of the black family and especially the diminished role of the father in the home. Their comments related to the black family are applicable to all families.

"At the root of most of the problems black people face is the breakdown of the family structure. Slightly over 70% of black children are raised in female-headed households. According to statistics about fatherless homes, 90% of homeless and runaway children are from fatherless homes; 71% of pregnant teenagers lack a father figure; 63% of youth suicides are from fatherless homes; 71% of high school dropouts come from fatherless homes; and 70% of juveniles in state-operated institutions have no father in the home. Furthermore, fatherless boys and girls are twice as likely to drop out of high school and twice as likely to end up in jail.

"One might say—

"Williams, one cannot ignore the legacy of slavery and the gross racism and denial of civil rights in yesteryear!"

"Let's look at whether black fatherless homes are a result of a "legacy of slavery" and racial discrimination. In the late 1800s, depending on the city, 70% to 80% of black households were two-parent. Dr. Thomas Sowell has argued, "The black family, which had survived centuries of slavery and discrimination, began rapidly disintegrating in the liberal welfare state that subsidized unwed pregnancy and changed welfare from an emergency rescue to a way of life."

"As late as 1950, only 18% of black households were single parent. From 1890 to 1940, a slightly higher percentage of black adults had married than white adults. In 1938, black illegitimacy was about 11% instead of today's 75%. In 1925, 85% of black households in New York City were two-parent. Today, the black family is a mere shadow of its past." ("Breakdown of the family structure, not racial discrimination, is the problem" by Walter Williams, *Tyler Morning Telegraph*, updated September 17, 2020)

This staggers the mind. Yet, God has told us all along that strong families are necessary to our well-being and to the rearing of children who will lead their own families. And who will in turn produce a strong nation. Note what God has said:

"Hear, O Israel: The Lord our God, the Lord is one. You shall love the Lord your God with all your heart and with all your soul and with all your might. And these words that I command you today shall be on your heart. You shall teach them diligently to your children, and shall talk of them when you sit in your house, and when you walk by the way, and when you lie down, and when you rise. You shall bind them as a sign on your hand, and they shall be as frontlets between your eyes. You shall write them on the doorposts of your house and on your gates (Deut. 6:4-9).

Husbands, love your wives, as Christ loved the church and gave himself up for her...Fathers do not provoke your children to anger, but bring them up in the discipline and instruction of the Lord (Ephesians 5:25a; 6:4).

The family is the key institution to all societies. If we want goodness and godliness in the People's House and the White House, it begins in our house.

2. The church – the absence of obedience to the "Great Commission."

Among the last words Jesus spoke on this earth were, *All authority in heaven and earth has been given to me. Go therefore and make disciples of all nations, baptizing them in the name of the Father, and of the Son and of the Holy Spirit, teaching them to observe all that I have commanded you. And behold, I am with you always, to the end of the age.* Matthew 28:18 - 20

"Nations" flows from the Greek term *ethen*, sometimes understood as people groups. The body of Christ is commissioned to reach all kinds of people groups. As contemporary believers are we obedient to the Great Commission or responsible for the demise of our culture due to great omission?

134

The church has pulled away from engagement. We might not be able to give a reason for the hope within us. We might fear the intrusion of the federal government that has the FBI treating Christians as terrorists. Even to the point of trying to infiltrate traditional Catholic congregations. How twisted is that?

Salt is useful and fulfills its purpose only if it comes into contact with a surface, a wound, or meat—to cleanse and to preserve. We have decided to cede the field and just keep the salt in the box. Jesus knew that salt was good only if it got out of the box. He told us to engage the world in order to share the gospel.

Paul said that we are engaged in a spiritual war. Just like the Roman soldier was trained to face the enemy, we should face our enemy. It is noteworthy that all the armor of the Roman soldier protected the front, not the back. Turn to run and the soldier was vulnerable. And once ground was gained, it was not yielded. Neither should we yield ground. We do not cede the field of battle. We do not wave the flag of surrender.

That is why Paul urged the Ephesian Christians to take up the whole armor of God and engage the enemy (Eph. 6:13). We then as soldiers of Christ are to stand firm.

3. Business/Finance – the absence of honesty.

A stanza in the poem, *Desiderata*, states a perceived truism:
Exercise caution in your business affairs, for the world is full of trickery. But let this not blind you to what virtue there is; many persons strive for high ideals, and everywhere life is full of heroism. (Max Ehrmann ©1927)

Exercise caution. Why? The world is full of trickery.

"Buyer beware." Have you ever heard the phrase? This might be the watchword for business affairs today. This warning and Max Ehrmann's directive are centered upon personal business affairs. But there might be a larger context in which business affairs affect our culture.

Let's consider a few phrases to help us center our thinking.

- Military Industrial Complex
- Scientific Industrial Complex
- Big Pharma
- Big Tech
- Global Corporations
- Bailouts
- Lobbyists
- Insider Trading

When we look at this list, we often have initial negative responses such as dishonest and unjust. These reactions are indicators of where the general public perception is of businesses today.

A friend was asked to look at this list and give an immediate response on what came to mind. His first word, "Corruption." Enough said.

We Are the Product

How many of us understand that we are the product? Our information. Our facetime before the various screens that fill our lives. We utilize "free" apps. Just go to the Play Store® and download. Only to have our information and our clicks sold to advertisers. If it is not behind a paywall, you are the product.

Nothing is free. The adage is "there still ain't no free lunch." Poor grammar but an eternal truth.

Our culture values things over people. Jesus never did.

We have probably all heard the old saying—"practice what you preach." Jesus didn't practice what He preached. He preached what He practiced. Jesus showed followers how to live, modeling three priorities.

1. The Priority of the Kingdom of God
2. The Priority of Persons over Things, even "Holy" Things
3. The Priority of Servanthood as a Way of Life

These are the core values of Jesus. These priorities of Jesus are diametrically opposed to the values and priorities of the world. His values should be the core values of His followers and the bases for all decisions—in personal relations and in business practices.

Think how the actions and teachings of Jesus revealed His priority of persons over things—even "holy" things.

- In Sychar, at Jacob's well, Jesus violated social mores. He conversed with a Samaritan woman.

- As a healer, Jesus willingly touched the "unclean": lepers, a woman who had hemorrhaged for twelve years, even dead bodies.

- Jesus welcomed children. The disciples, on the other hand, tried to deter them.

- On the Sabbath, Jesus exorcised a demon at the synagogue in Capernaum; He also healed a man whose right hand had withered, another man afflicted with dropsy, and an arthritic woman too stiff to stand upright.

- On the Sabbath, Jesus let the disciples pluck grain and eat. The Twelve feasted more, fasted less (Mt. 9:14-17). They ate but skipped ritual hand washings (Mark 7:1-13).

Valuing persons above things actually led to the death of Jesus. A little noticed passage reveals how Jesus healing a man on the Sabbath led to the collusion of opposing forces who felt threatened by Him. *And he looked around at them with anger, grieved at their hardness of heart, and said to the man, "Stretch out your hand." He stretched it out, and his hand was restored. The Pharisees went out and immediately held counsel with the Herodians against him, how to destroy him* (Mark 3:5-6).

The Pharisees mixed religious zeal and political clout effectively. Ambition, popularity, and control had seduced the Pharisees. As a result, they opposed anyone (1) contesting their authority or (2) disputing their credibility. Jesus did both publicly.

His criticism of and conflict with the Jewish leadership would lead to His death.

Paul warned that the love of money (*philargyria*) is the root of all evil (1 Tim. 6:10). The love of money will lead you to use people and value things. Think of the issues so destructive to humanity—war, drugs, pornography, human trafficking of women and children, gambling, additions of all kinds. These are all driven by the love of money and the use of people.

Jesus valued persons above things. How would He evaluate our culture and, especially, our business culture? Remember His warning about values—*For what shall it profit a man, if he shall gain the whole world, and lose his own soul: Or what will a man give in exchange for his soul* (Mark 8:36-37 Webster Bible Translation)*?*

4. The government – the absence of integrity.

Placing hands on a copy of the Scriptures, our federal officials pledge an "oath of office." Jesus warned about the pitfalls of committing to an oath. He summarizes, *Let what you say be simply, 'Yes' or 'No'; anything more than this comes from evil* (Mt. 5:37).

It's a simple issue of integrity. It is evil and deceptive for our elected officials to pledge oaths of integrity and then violate them.

For federal civil service employees, the oath is set forth by law in 5 U.S. Code § 3331, which reads as follows:

"An individual, except the President, elected or appointed to an office of honor or profit in the civil service or uniformed services, shall take the following oath: *"I, ___, do solemnly swear (or affirm) that I will support and defend the Constitution of the United States against all enemies, foreign and domestic; that I will bear true faith and allegiance to the same; that I take this obligation freely,*

138

without any mental reservation or purpose of evasion; and that I will well and faithfully discharge the duties of the office on which I am about to enter. So help me God.'"

The President takes the following oath of office: *"I do solemnly swear (or affirm) that I will faithfully execute the Office of President of the United States, and will to the best of my Ability, preserve, protect and defend the Constitution of the United States."*

One commentator has said about these oaths, "The oath is to support and defend the U.S. Constitution and faithfully execute your duties. The intent is to protect the public from a government that might fall victim to political whims and to provide a North Star—the Constitution—as a source of direction."

The Constitution was written to restrict government. Unless specified in the Constitution, the powers and privileges are retained by the states and by individuals.

The purpose of government is to protect the citizens who are under the care of the government. The government is to punish the wrongdoers. This is the measure of good government. How is ours measuring up to that standard? Is the government protecting the law-abiding citizens and punishing those who break the law? It really is a simple test.

We have moved from being under the protection of government to being under the thumb of government.

Every important building block of our culture has been underpinned by an oath beginning with the family—when a man and a woman exchange vows. The court system, the military, government service of all kinds, even legalized immigrants—all take an oath. But when people do not live up to their oaths, justice is perverted.

And the darkness of injustice descends. The darkness intensifies in America today. The list of injustices continues to grow. But let's highlight just one—the invasion across our southern border.

Invasion

The Roman Empire came to near collapse in the third century A.D. We listed a variety of the reasons for the near-collapse on page 108. One of the reasons was the invasion across the northern Rhine border of the western Roman Empire and across the Danube border of the eastern Empire. The Germanic tribes pushed into the territories of the Empire. They were driven back by emperors Aurelian and, later, by Diocletian in the third century. But they would return.

In A.D. 406, the Rhine River froze over. It allowed a massive number of the barbarian tribes to flood into what is today France, Spain, and northern Africa. Within 70 years (A.D. 476), the western Roman Empire would fall to them. In three generations, control of the western Empire was lost.

Now, America is facing its own invasion. Six million+ "known" illegals have crossed into our land in the last three years. (Some experts on illegal immigration put the figure at twice that.) And that number does not account for the got-aways—and who knows who they are. Good judgement has to assume that those who avoid the border patrol (who is turning practically nobody back) have nefarious reasons to want to be in America. They are law-breakers by the sheer act of crossing the border. But those who avoid detection bring criminal and terrorist dangers to our country.

Todd Bensman, Texas-based Senior National Security Fellow for the Center for Immigration Studies (CIS) writes and speaks about the nexus between immigration and national security. Bensman reports that illegals from over 170 countries have crossed our southern border. Many are military-aged men from "countries of national security concern." This designation means that people from these countries require enhanced terrorism-security screening. It took only 19 terrorists to give us 9-11. Now, more than 7,300 immigrants from dozens of these countries deemed national security concerns have crossed into our country during the period of May 2021 through August 2023. Since 2021, a record-breaking 270 illegal border-crossers on the FBI terrorism watch list have been apprehended. These are the ones we know. The got aways are not listed among this number. (Todd Bensman with Center for Immigration Studies; House of Representatives Judiciary Report on Border Crisis, January 18, 2024)

Congressman Glenn Grothman (WI-06) reports in an article entitled, *Chaos at the Southern Border*— "Border Patrol is estimating 600,000 got aways this fiscal year (2022), up from their report of 365,200 in FY 2021 and 118,848 in FY 2020. (If we follow this trajectory, the number is over a million and a half got aways in the last three years.)

"Leaving the door open for anyone in the world to enter our country unlawfully encourages drug smugglers and human traffickers to take advantage of our broken immigration protocols. The Biden Administration's neglect has served as a gateway to heinous abuses against women and children at the hands of criminal drug cartels, who are generating billions in profits.

"Without necessary resources from Washington, Border Patrol faces the immense challenge to detect and confiscate deadly drugs during this nonstop rush of illegal immigrants. As a result of the President's open-border agenda, fentanyl and other lethal substances are streaming into American communities, which tragically led to over 100,000 dying by overdose last year alone." (https://grothman.house.gov/news/documentsingle.aspx?DocumentID=3192)

We could take a lesson from a plague that swept across Europe in the 1300's. Called "The Black Death," bubonic plague became the first great pandemic. This devastating global crisis originated in (are you ready for this) China! This disease traveled on global trade routes. Also, power-hungry leaders weaponized "The Black Death" using infested rats to kill, weaken, and defeat their enemies.

Any parallels here? Considering that little is known of the health history of the illegals, it can be assured diseases such as measles, mumps, small pox, and chicken pox are reintroduced into our culture. Nor should we wonder where lung diseases like tuberculosis originated. And we should not wonder at the rise of drug-related deaths and even a ramp up of terrorist attacks on our homeland.

Is it not amazing that Americans have been kept from all kinds of community and inter-personal engagements and interaction because they were not vaccinated in the recent Covid pandemic? Yet, at the southern border all diseases are magically left behind in Mexico. The illegals are passed right on through, loaded on buses and planes, and delivered to cities all across the country. No vaccinations required. Do not be surprised when diseases we thought irradicated in America have a resurrection. Express no shock at the conquering of the nation.

Overpowering the Western Roman Empire took just three generations, 70 years, by the Germanic tribal invasion. Overpowering America will take far less time. The invasion of our nation is occurring at a much more rapid pace. The tools and efficiencies have all been enhanced. And our government is financing the invasion.

Does this sound like a government protecting its citizens? Does this sound like policies put in place by people who have taken oaths to *preserve, protect, and defend the Constitution of the United States*? Injustice rages.

Border canaries are being ignored today in this modern-day invasion. It is time for accountability. It is time for sentinels to arise.

Steps to take now:

Action # 1: Visit with your church's leadership to discover what is being done to support the men and fathers in your church and community.

Action # 2: Call your representatives for action to control our borders, remove every person who entered our country illegally, and follow immigration laws already in place.

Action # 3: Insist that your representative support finishing the wall along our southern border.

Chapter Eight
When a Nation Turns Away

The difference between "opinions" and "facts" continues to be confusing and a source of contention in our culture. A growing tendency in our nation is to allow baseless, even moronic, opinions to prevail over established absolutes.

The easiest example that fills the headlines today is the "trans" epidemic. It appears to be a social contagion. Look at the following graphs. They are from a variety of sources. They are limited in the years covered in most instances. They are to provide you only with an impression.

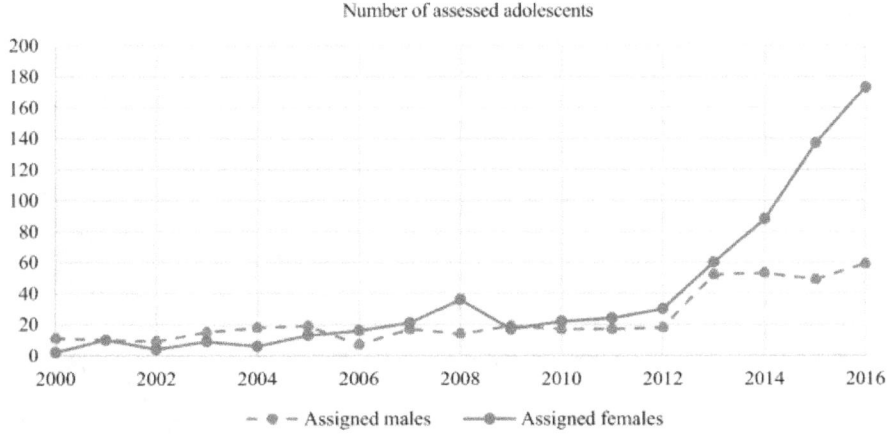

Number of assessed adolescents

- ● - Assigned males ─●─ Assigned females

Arnoldussen, M., Steensma, T.D., Popma, A. et al. Re-evaluation of the Dutch approach: are recently referred transgender youth different compared to earlier referrals?. Eur Child Adolesc Psychiatry 29, 803–811 (2020). https://doi.org/10.1007/s00787-019-01394-6

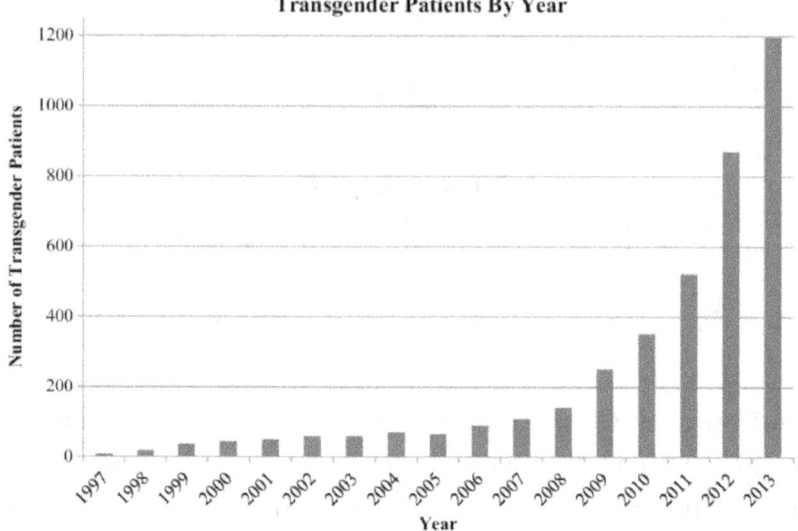

Data Note: Figure displays active transgender patients by calendar year. "Active" is defined as a patient who had a visit in that calendar year and accessed the transgender health program (documented in their electronic medical record) before the end of that calendar year.

Figure 1: Pediatric patient referrals* to specialist clinics for hormone treatment for gender identity issues: Nine Canadian clinics

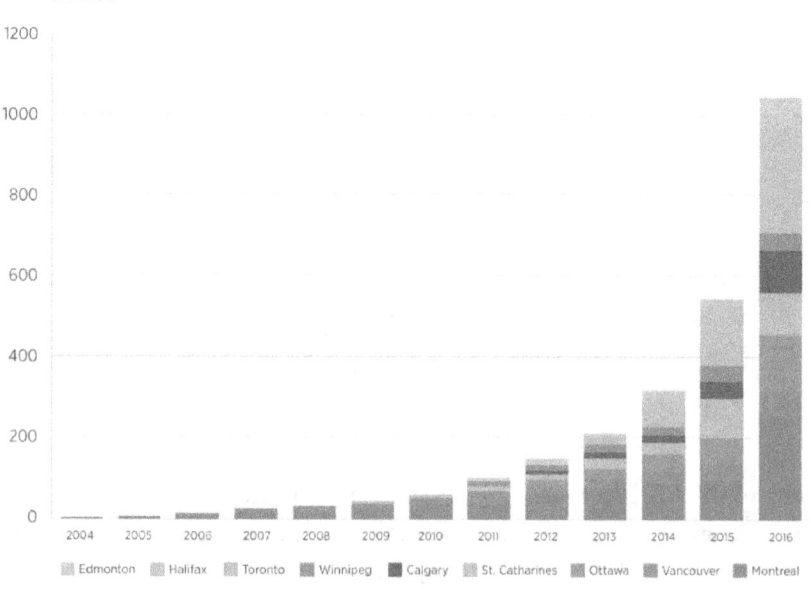

*some referral numbers estimated
Source: Canadian Gender Report 2019

Cumulative Total of People Who Officially Changed Their Gender

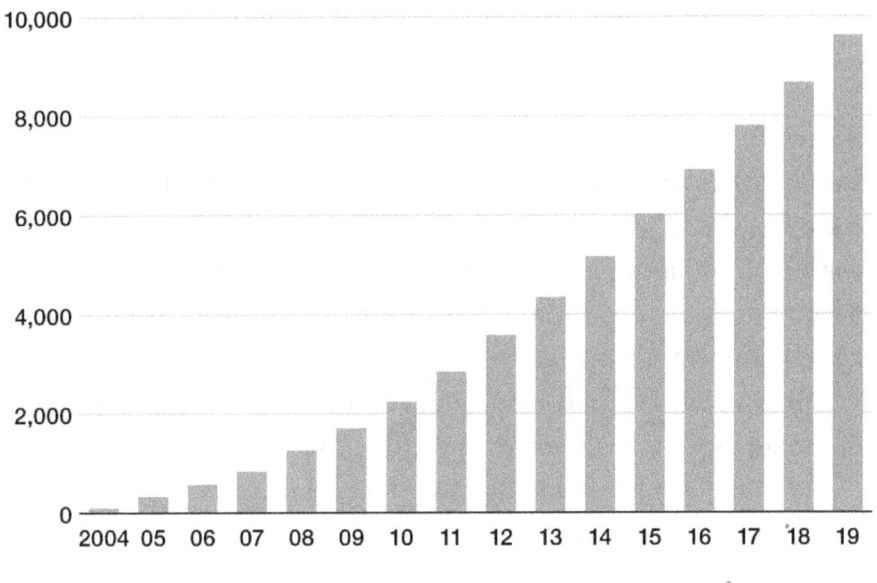

Created by *Nippon.com* based on judicial statistics.

Referrals to the gender identity development service, by gender assigned at birth   (UK)

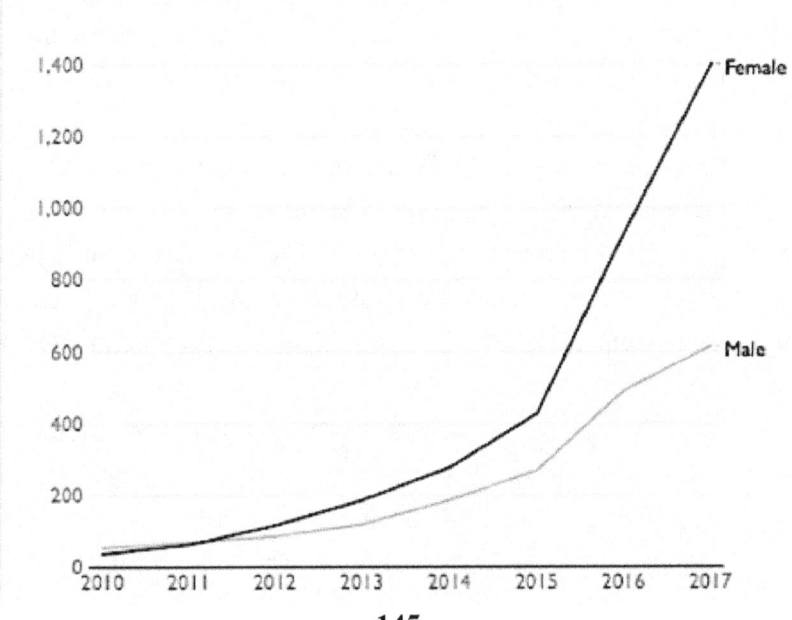

When you look at these charts certain indicators emerge:

- As late as 2000, the reported cases are practically nil.
- Beginning around 2012, the number of cases rises dramatically.
- More girls than boys report transgender issues.

Some of these reports are limited in scope and population. For instance, the re-evaluation survey was of the Dutch population. The Canadian study was from nine clinics spread across Canada. One chart is from Japan. One is from the U.K. (We would have liked to have referenced a chart from the Center for Disease Control, but it has reported limited research on this topic.)

But in every chart, the marked rise came after 2009-2010. Some are especially abrupt around 2012. Why?

We might suggest that the rise of social networks played a part. The prevalence of smart phones and the broad distribution of them in the adolescent population might have played a part. The notoriety of various high profile transitioning role models could have played a part. Is something else at play? Food additives? We cannot know. But what we can say is that the rise has been notable in recent years.

And, although we were unable to reflect a chart of transgenderism in America, we can say confidently that what is happening in other cultures is happening here. And maybe at a more alarming rate.

In a July 2021 survey, the Pew Research Center found:
"At a time when a rising share of U.S. adults say they know someone who is transgender, there is no public consensus on whether greater social acceptance of transgender people is good or bad for society, according to a Pew Research Center survey conducted last July.

"A stark difference exists between Republicans and Democrats on this topic, and views also vary among some key demographic groups, including groups within each party.

"A majority of Democrats and those who lean toward the Democratic Party (59%) say that the greater acceptance of transgender people is good for society, while a majority of Republicans and Republican leaners (54%) say it is bad for society. Republicans are also slightly more likely than Democrats to say it's neither good nor bad.

"By ideology, the differences are even more dramatic. Three-quarters of liberal Democrats say greater acceptance of transgender people has been good for society. This compares with 45% of moderate or conservative Democrats, 27% of moderate or liberal Republicans and just 8% of conservative Republicans. Meanwhile, 65% of conservative Republicans say acceptance of trans people has been bad for society, while just 6% of liberal Democrats say the same."

("Deep partisan divide on whether greater acceptance of transgender people is good for society" by Anna Brown, Pew Research Center, February 11, 2022, https://www.pewresearch.org)

The Christian community will generally see this expression of individual sexual identity negatively. They would see this as having a detrimental effect upon our culture and especially be seen as an unhealthy model for children who are forming their own views and expressions of their sexuality. The Christian community allows for personal behavior choices. Choice, after all, is at the core of both sin and salvation. But they are also guided by what they would say are divine directives for public and personal behavior in relation to the society as a whole. More about this in a bit.

Off the Rails

- When mediocre male athletes are allowed to identify as female to compete in women's sports, something has gone off the rails.
- When a nominee to the Supreme Court cannot define "woman," something has gone off the rails.
- When debauchery is flaunted in the streets before children, something has gone off the rails.

- When something that is clearly mutilation and child abuse is called "gender-affirming care," something has gone off the rails.

- When parents are threatened with having their children removed because they refer to them by their birth gender, something has gone off the rails.

- When misgendering someone or not using the desired pronoun for a person becomes a crime punishable by imprisonment for up to two years or a fine up to $5,000, or both, something has gone off the rails.

- When schools can use a different name and pronoun for a student without a parent's permission, something has gone off the rails.

- When doctors can prescribe puberty blockers and other "transgender health care" procedures for minors without parental consent, something has gone off the rails.

And this list can go on and on. Why are we here? Because of a failure to accept authority—the real authority, the word of God.

It gets really simple. *So God created humankind in his image, in the image of God he created them; male and female he created them* (Genesis 1:27 New Revised Standard Version). To deal with basic biology for just a moment—it comes down to chromosomes—XX or XY. Forensic anthropologists can dig up skeletons thousands of years old and tell which was a man and which was a woman. Why? Because of skeletal structure.

Sex/gender is typically determined by the morphology (shape) of the pelvis or skull and long bone measurements. Especially useful is the pelvis structure because of adaptations for child bearing. Men and women are built differently. It is by design. It is drawn into the blueprint of life itself. And it has not been altered since the proto-type.

Are their exceptions? Yes. A couple of variant, atypical sex chromosome patterns are notable. One is Klinefelter's syndrome

(XXY) which effects one in every 750 males. The other is Turner syndrome (X with one X missing or incomplete) which effects one in every 2,200 females. But when these are considered as percentages of the population, the instances are infinitesimal. These variants in the physiology do not explain the rise in transgenderism. The rise can only be explained as part of a mass psychosis.

Drivers

What is driving this increase in diagnoses? Here is a picture:

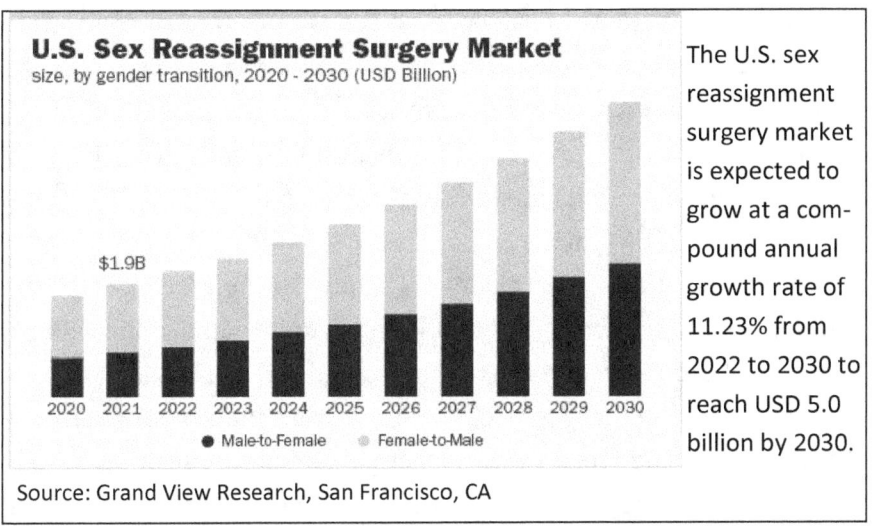

U.S. Sex Reassignment Surgery Market
size, by gender transition, 2020 - 2030 (USD Billion)

$1.9B

2020 2021 2022 2023 2024 2025 2026 2027 2028 2029 2030

● Male-to-Female   ○ Female-to-Male

The U.S. sex reassignment surgery market is expected to grow at a compound annual growth rate of 11.23% from 2022 to 2030 to reach USD 5.0 billion by 2030.

Source: Grand View Research, San Francisco, CA

Not to be too cynical—but one of the apparent drivers of the trend toward sex reassignment surgery appears to be profit. And the money train doesn't stop with the surgery. Life-long patients are being created. Because the "care" goes on and on. To quote the good book, *for the love of money is the root of all evil*. Is that too cynical?

But the profit driver is not the only driver. This becomes a wedge issue, splitting the country in more and more ways. And if political advantage can be gained, it will be used. Is that too cynical?

The social contagion within the teen community is rather typical of other types of behaviors that have afflicted teens over the years. What is different this time is the lack of parental involvement

149

in the lives of children. Or, in some cases, the active push of parents to inflict the psychosis and delusion on their children.

For instance, an illustrative case is of one mother who has two children—an older son and a younger daughter. She has tried incessantly to make her son a homosexual and to transition her daughter into a boy. How sick does a parent have to be to impose this confusion on her children? Can this not be considered child abuse? Not in today's perverted landscape. It now is called "gender affirming care." God might call it by another name.

But some parents are concerned for the welfare of their children. They are concerned that Critical Race Theory is being taught making their children hate their own race. Concerned that males are being allowed to share the girls' bathrooms and gym dressing rooms. That their daughters are having to compete with male athletes claiming to be females.

A young girl in the Loudoun County Virginia school system was sexually assaulted by a boy claiming to be female and having access to the girls' bathrooms. The school hid the assault. When the girl's father demanded accountability from the school board, he was arrested. And when these concerned parents show up to school board meetings, they are treated as terrorist threats by the FBI. That is where we are. Madness has taken over.

The Last Stages

This attack on our children is one of the more evil movements destroying families today. Some teachers and schools assist children to begin a "social" transitioning by calling children by another name or identifying them by another pronoun other than one appropriate to the child's birth gender. These people infringe upon parental rights and responsibilities. But their action is just one part of this evil ideology taking aim at the heart of the family and, on a larger scale, the destruction of our culture.

Camille Paglia, academician and avowed liberal, has stated that from her research into cultures around the world, androgyny is one of the last stages of a culture in collapse. She especially highlighted the collapse of the Greek and Roman cultures. She drew attention to the works of art and the depiction they made of the forms of men and women.

How are our art works (including movies) portraying men and women to our current culture? Are our arts merely a reflection of the culture? Or do they shape the culture? If the latter, who is deciding what gets produced? Who determines the content to which your children are exposed?

This last question is more indicting than we might imagine. Because it is the parents to whom God gave the responsibility to teach their children (Deut. 6:6-8). It might demand greater involvement in the training up of our children. We might have to make more concerted, intentional efforts at instilling our values into the lives of our children. We might have to be more protective and discerning of the threats to the health and well-being of our developing children. We are guides and protectors as well as their providers.

Authority

Authority, specifically biblical authority, and opinion are diametrically opposite terms. "Opinions," Webster says, is "a view of judgment formed about something, not necessarily based on fact or knowledge."

"Authority," is "power to influence or command thought, opinion or behavior." Like having a steering wheel to a car or a rudder to a ship, when a nation embraces biblical authority, it is able to navigate through multiple moral messes rather than enduring them.

The culture becomes morally and spiritually handicapped where absolutes are absent. The Bible identifies this moral demise as "strongholds." Paul encountered these strongholds when he came into Greece on his missionary journeys. The Greeks prided themselves on their erudite enlightenment. Paul met this arrogance on

Mars Hill in Athens. Later, Paul would write the infant congregation of Corinthian Christians about a spiritual truth—*the god of this world has blinded the minds of the unbelieving* (2 Cor. 4:4). Sadly, even deceived people continually yearn for direction.

In the last words Paul wrote, he warned his assistant, Timothy: *For the time is coming when people will not endure sound teaching, but having itching ears they will accumulate for themselves teachers to suit their own passions, and will turn away from listening to the truth and wander off into myths* (2 Timothy 4: 3-4).

So where do they turn? They conform to baseless, unfounded opinions. Their opinions being shaped by a variety of culprits in this decaying culture. Culprits include:

Political Pundits

These people are attached to both sides of the legislative isle. Countless millions of dollars are funneled to these pundits so that both political parties may form "planks" in their political platforms.

Listening to these "talking heads" can be a head-splitting, hopeless activity.

Hollywood and New York City

The coastal centers of what passes for culture are overweighted by money and media. The movie industry is saturated heavily by wicked men and women who seek to control our culture. Years ago, what was once a subliminal thought, now is blatantly "in your face." Same is true for many media/television products. Both flow from an industry that lacks a moral compass. The only "true north" these entities have is money and power. Deceived, deranged people can only lead gullible viewers if allowed.

Professional Athletes

Professional sports is a seedbed of baseless opinion. The NBA, NFL, even the Olympics have "opinion that is not based on the facts." Do you recall when the NFL capitulated to athletes who refused to stand during the singing of the National Anthem? Men and women who were making millions of dollars knelt in protest of our nation and our culture. Meanwhile, their supporters ignorantly rushed to watch them perform. Some NBA players wore T-shirts in warmups that said, "Black Lives Matter." Yet, they refused to condemn China for their slave-labor camps where their over-priced merchandise is made. Some lives must matter more than others. These hypocrites are bought with thirty pieces of silver.

Pundits, arrogant actors, and professional athletes too often share opinions whether the viewing audience wants to listen or not! Wouldn't it be satisfying to say to pundits, "If we want your opinion, we will give it to you."

We pay to watch prima-donna athletes bounce, catch, throw, or protect a ball. That is the extent of the intelligence many of these people offer to a hungry, searching culture.

What about media and movies? The content offered is filled with endless sexual overtones, vile language, and open displays of deviant living. We are being incessantly pounded with values that are diametrically opposed to God and His values. And these "values" are detrimental to the well-being of our citizens, our culture, our country.

The words of Laura Ingraham, "shut up and sing," ring true here. The canaries in our culture are looking for moments of escape in media. They are not wanting to be ensnared.

Trusted direction, not opinions, is the need of the day. Our nation is drowning in a moral cesspool. It's unnecessary. It's a choice. New depths of shocking perversion are being explored continually. Like water seeking the lowest possible level, a depraved culture struggles with defining moral and ethical issues. Like a rudderless ship, our nation cannot navigate these issues because biblical ideals are being erased, modified, or restructured by subtle influences of a depraved nature.

If we think sectors of our culture are bad today, just give a few years and see how degenerate the fallen become. Bounce forward one generation. We should not be surprised to hear that future generation pine for the "good old days of the 2020's."

Recently a man who describes himself as an agnostic commented, "It seems that the gates of hell have been opened on America." That is what happens when a nation or a people are turned over to *a reprobate mind*. They spiral deeper and deeper into depravity. Paul described the degradation of humanity in Romans 1:18-32:

> *And since they did not see fit to acknowledge God, God gave them up to a debased mind to do what ought not to be done. They were filled with all manner of unrighteousness, evil, covetousness, malice. They are full of envy, murder, strife, deceit, maliciousness. They are gossips, slanderers, haters of God, insolent, haughty, boastful, inventors of evil, disobedient to parents, foolish, faithless, heartless, ruthless. Though they know God's righteous decree that those who practice such things deserve to die, they not only do them but give approval to those who practice them.*

The description is of the fatal direction of a culture in free-fall. It aptly applies to our current culture. We're bad and getting worse! However, there are many contemporary canaries who fearlessly warn those who have chosen a lifestyle with morals that make an ally cat blush.

What are some indicators of a culture in free fall?

1. Same words, different dictionaries

In *1984*, George Orwell gave birth to the premise "Big Brother is Watching." That means our government is observing us as citizens. It has the goal of catching us engaging in or fomenting some action they label as seditious. Overcoming lawful freedom of expression begins by controlling the spoken and written word. Control the language, control the truth.

"He who controls the language controls the masses."
–Saul Alinsky, *Rules for Radicals*

In George Orwell's *1984*, language takes a key role in determining culture.

Michael Brown, Ph.D. in Near Eastern Languages and Literatures, quoted a post about the need to control language based on *1984*: "By controlling the language, Big Brother controls the way that the people think. With a limited vocabulary, the people are limited in how much they can think, as well as, what they think about."

Brown concluded, "Those who control the language control the culture." (christianpost.com, Michael Brown, "Those who control the language control the culture", September 10, 2020)

The transfer of truth comes through communication. The medium is language, which is in constant flux. As knowledge expands in our culture, so should our language. Just think about the language of technology in communication. First came telegraphic abilities. On the heels of that "new" technology was the telephone. For decades that phone was attached to a wall. Then came the introduction of a cell phone, texting with emojis, Facebook® and Twitter® accounts. The progression of communication mediums is undeniable.

With all these advances, we have failed to consider the fact that certain segments of our culture are unable to keep pace with all the changes of communication. This is by design. For example, linguistic engineering begins control by disallowing certain kinds of speech. Signs and books are banned that do not meet the approval of the controlling body. Stiff penalties are incurred by those in the culture who violate this movement.

Free speech is essential to a free society. This is why the First Amendment incorporates freedom of speech. Currently, speech is a battle ground for many of the headline cases being brought by the Department of Justice and investigative arms like the FBI. This is where freedom is lost. One case at a time.

A few examples of how power is seized include:

- In 1962, the Supreme Court ruled that school mandated prayers in public schools to be unconstitutional. Today, that ruling has morphed into students not having the ability to pray in public schools—period. Some students are objects of ridicule when carrying a copy of the Scriptures to class. However, there are canaries in this coal mine too! Consider the stance of Joseph Kennedy, a Washington state high school football coach who lost his job after leading students in a midfield prayer session after games. His boldness is to be applauded.

Kennedy won a 1.7-million-dollar settlement and retained his coaching position the following year.

- A concerted effort to remove the Ten Commandments has spread like wildfire in our culture. Interestingly, these faithful laws are referenced in the highest court of the land, the Supreme Court, but has been removed from public view across the nation. Our Supreme Court has the representation of these statutes in clear view. Our children are not afforded the same privilege.

When timeless principles like "you shall not kill" are eradicated from social conversation, it should not be surprising that the next step is to murder the unborn. America has the blood of more than 63,000,000 aborted babies on her hands since 1973. This blatant attack on the womb continues by "redefining" what a baby is. However, in spite of research that shows a child's heart beats at 21 days and audible at 8-10 weeks of gestation, there are some who reject the moral implications biblical authority brings to every culture.

Today it is abortion. Tomorrow, it may be forced euthanasia of the sick, poor, or nonproductive sectors of our society. And when life becomes meaningless, when we are seen as just a clump of cells, when life itself is viewed as a cosmic accident—is it any wonder that murder is rampant in the streets and our schools become shooting galleries?

Control the language, control the truth, control the culture!

- Attack on the message of a local church. More than 350,000 various congregations are in operation today. Pressures are mounting to conform to cultural changes and it will not be long before pastors of every denomination will be incarcerated for speaking against any social abnormalities. Such speech will be deemed "hate crimes."

Ten years have passed since the Canadian Supreme Court ruled that biblical language opposing homosexual behavior, including speaking as well as in written form, is essentially a crime. These judges believe that this kind of language targets homosexuals. One dissident, William Whatcott, was sued by two homosexuals for $7,500 who were offended with the flyers he distributed. Also, the Canadian Human Rights Commission demanded that Whatcott pay hundreds of thousands of dollars in fines.

This will have a direct effect on church membership and attendance by homosexual groups who attend simply to force the conversation away from their deviant lifestyle. Churches and their leaders should brace to be challenged in courts that have been influenced with subtle changes in cultural language.

Because depravity never stops in a culture, we should not be surprised with the rise in transexual/pansexual/polysexual behavior, cross dressing, transgenderism, pedophilia, and human trafficking. How does a culture reach such ever-deepening depths?

2. The rejection of authority

The cultural demise of our society is the result of rejecting any form of authority or redefining it. Redefining something occurs when similar terminology is employed but the terms flow from different dictionaries. Plans are afoot in some arenas to steal written and verbal communication from us. This blatant move applies continual pressure for redefining words. One term that is challenged on three different fronts is "authority."

157

Authority in the heart

A shift from revelation to reason is rampant in our culture. Whether in the world of science, philosophy, or within the mindset of people, authority has become the result of the mind of man rather than the mind of God. Proverbs 14:12 warns, *There is a way that seems right to a man, but its end is the way of death.*

Every person is a soul. He/she does not have a soul—they are a soul. Every soul contains emotional, logical, and volitional dimensions. Our emotional dimension includes love and anger; our logical dimension is the thinking side of us. The volitional dimension is how we make choices in life.

When authority is based on the mind of man the results may include rationalizing racism toward legitimate cultures. Furthermore, we then "justify" our logic of racism and finally we choose to oppose people different from us. However, when authority is based on the mind of God, we gain His perspective on our thinking, feelings, and choices in life.

For example, no city, county, or state can afford a police officer on every street corner. However, authority, based on a biblical world view is in action because we know that each person is afforded his or her basic sanctity of life. Nearly all cultures recognize the value of life and the offense of taking a life. Big Brother is absent, but authority is present. This is what Paul referred to in Roman 2:14 -15—the inward, natural law of conscience. Knowing right from wrong. Justifying behavior that tears down culture, finds its roots in a lack of authority within one's heart.

Authority in the home

The home is fundamental to building society. Within that home are parents who are commissioned to rear their children to become self-dependent and productive citizens. The nurturing of a mother and the leadership offered by a father are critical to every developing child. Take one of the two out of the equation and we have a recipe for a dysfunctional culture.

Attacks on the family structure are relentless. Media often portrays men as weak members of the home. That subliminal message from movies, commercials, music, print adds to further dysfunction and the home becomes a relic of the past. Parents soon lose their "say" in how their children are reared.

Parental rights were at the forefront of a recent gubernatorial election in Virginia. During a debate, the Democrat nominee, Terry McAuliffe, insisted that parents should have no role in directing the education of their children. Glenn Youngkin promoted parental involvement and control. Youngkin won!

When parents in Fairfax County, Virginia learned of sexually explicit content in two books that were available to children in the school library, Stacy Langton took matters into her own hands as she stood at a podium during a school board meeting quoting Virginia Code 18.2-376: *"It shall be unlawful for any person knowingly to... circulate... any notice or advertisement of any obscene item..."*

Control the language, control the truth, control the culture.

Remember that Loudoun County Virginia incident mentioned earlier—it was another demonstration of how the family is being systematically dismantled by liberal members controlling local school boards. Scott Smith attended a board meeting looking for answers to why action was not taken to deal with a sexual assault on his daughter by a 14 year-old boy. After heated debate with members of the school board, Smith was arrested for "domestic terrorism."

What action was taken? Loudoun County Virginia has developed a pilot project that includes building all gender, single occupancy bathrooms in five schools. The cost to tax payers will exceed 11 million dollars.

Where is the influence of fathers today? According to Pew Research Center—

- 37% of white children are born outside wedlock.
- 72% of black children are born outside wedlock.

- 59% of Hispanic children are born outside wedlock.

This means young men and women do not have a role model to learn from and duplicate as they move into adulthood. Just think how many social ills would be solved when men commit to rearing children they fathered. Being an absentee dad is a growing trend that must be curbed.

Revival will come to this country's families when fathers return to the home. Doug TenNapel posted this from Save Your Sons—

More good dads = less crime
More good dads = less poverty
More good dads = less violence
More good dads = less illiteracy
More good dads = less dropouts
More good dads = less addiction
More good dads = less self-harm
More good dads = less child abuse
More good dads = less sexual abuse
More good dads = less mental illness
More good dads = less homelessness
More good dads = less teen pregnancy
More good dads = less government dependence

More good dads = a better world in every way

SaveYourSons@save.your.sons

The family has always been the cornerstone of our culture and not just ours but all cultures. Families preserve and pass on values to succeeding generations we all need. Without this basic building block, our culture will continue her free-fall.

Authority in the homeland

The framers of the Constitution declared in their opening statement that, "all Men…are endowed by their Creator with certain unaliena-ble Rights."

Montana State Senator and historian, John Fuller provides insight into the application of authority, specifically on the federal level. During a recent interview, Senator Fuller noted that the original use of the word, "inalienable" was "in-a-lien-able." The concept is that no one is able to retain or hold in possession the property of another person until a debt is paid. The application is that "no lien can be put on our rights." They are granted by the Creator and these rights are unable to be held hostage by anyone or taken away for any reason.

Because of the protections afforded by the Constitution, authority at any governmental level, especially the federal government, is never seized. That authority is granted by the people and exists for the people. Citizens do not have to bow before a king nor do we pledge allegiance to a person. The authority we give our representatives is in our hands through our vote.

We live in critical times as a nation. These times have been exacerbated by Christians who have refused to vote. Often our choices are not black and white. They are often gray. The lesser of two evils. But by sitting out the election, we have given control of our nation into the hands of those who oppose the causes of good and God. By yielding the field of battle, we have given easy victories to forces of darkness. The results have been disastrous. By now many of us have figured out that elections do have consequences.

What are some of the consequences of giving authority to the current administration?

- Our southern border has been overwhelmed.

- Our economy is floundering under excessive federal government spending. The stimulation packages are hitting our economy with sugar highs. Each one is piling up the national debt. We do not have the money. We are borrowing at record rates.

- Where once we were energy independent and even exporting oil to other countries, today our national leaders travel to Middle-eastern nations begging for additional oil production.

The United States maintains a Strategic Petroleum Reserve at four sites on the Gulf of Mexico. The total capacity of this reserve is 727 million barrels of crude oil. Under current administration leadership our national reserve is the lowest in almost 40 years. Energy prices have increased by more than 40% and are the highest in 15 years.

- The Chinese habitually steal intellectual properties and purchase vast tracts of farmland in America, some of which are located near our nuclear defense systems. We are in what the Chinese have called an Unrestricted War. Not only Unrestricted but also *un-resisted* by our leadership. When our "leaders" receive million-dollar payments from China, should we expect push-back?

- Over-regulation is stealing our freedom and self-agency. The administrative state is reaching its tenacles into every crack and crevice of our lives. It is coming for everything from gas ranges to gun braces to gas-burning vehicles. The list goes on and on.

The effects of the abuse of authority by an unhinged federal government is felt by every citizen in our nation. When will any canary voice be heard?

Famed coach Vince Lombardi once held up a football to his team of professionals and said, "This is a football." That's simplification indeed! Here is a suggestion for helping our federal government simplify their processes as well as reign in their abuses of power. Begin by delivering the mail and protecting our borders. After those two items are operating efficiently, then move to another "complicated" issue.

Also, because of the absence or abuses of authority, it seems our culture is developing the morals of ancient Rome. New depths of shocking perversion are being explored continually. It's called "depravity."

Every culture struggles with defining morality issues. Like water seeking the lowest possible levels to flow, often, morals descend to lower levels. Today's moral ideals are being erased, modified, or restructured by the influences of a depraved nature.

When we hear the words <u>Sodom</u> and <u>Gomorrah</u>, we focus only upon the depravity as the reason for their destruction. A little recognized statement by the prophet Ezekiel puts a remarkable twist on the story of destruction—*As I live, declares the Lord God, your sister Sodom and her daughters have not done as you and your daughters have done. Behold, this was the guilt of your sister Sodom: she and her daughters had pride, excess of food, and prosperous ease, but did not aid the poor and needy. They were haughty and did an abomination before me. So I removed them, when I saw it* (Ezekiel 16:48-50).

God's evaluation could apply equally well to America:
- pride
- excess food
- prosperous ease
- no aid to the poor and needy
- haughty
- debauched

Verdict: removed.

3. The hypocrisy of the Intolerant

Tolerance once meant that another's beliefs and opinions were acknowledged without being pressured to endorse or accept them. However, today, our culture is being pushed to accept a redefinition of tolerance. Basically, tolerance now requires everyone to accept every subjective belief as valid. This is at the heart of the phrase, "my personal truth." It includes that every individual has the right to their own moral code which cannot be judged by others. Judging is "intolerant." Any questioning voices must be shut out of the marketplace of thought and closed out from logical dialogue.

Remember, there is nothing new under the sun. The Book of Judges describes one of the darkest and longest times in Old Testament history. Some 450 years that extended from Joshua's conquest of the Promised Land until the time of Samuel, the last judge and first prophet of Israel. That era was saturated with bloody conflicts, horrific acts of wickedness, and stories of human misery. Absolute moral chaos was the rule of these days.

During these 450 years, God raised up 12 canaries, known as Judges to call the nation to repentance. Like a roller-coaster, the nation repented and then returned to their own wicked ways in time. The cycle was repeated time and time again.

Two verses in Judges (17:6; 21:25) sum up the cause of the nation's misery: *Everyone did what was right in his own eyes.*

Today, the new phrase is, "just follow your heart" or "this is my truth." At the root of this warped thinking is the absence of absolutes. If someone denies standards that are fixed and righteous (like the Ten Commandments), then they have no moral obligation to follow those standards. That's why Solomon states, *The way of a fool is right in his own eyes* (Proverbs 12:15).

It's been almost ten years since Wendy Kaminar, a lawyer and writer warned that, "…contemporary liberalism involves a virtual embrace of censorship; a therapeutic approach to rights; very expansive definitions of harm; and hostility to freedom of speech, conscience, and belief."

Our culture is being conditioned to adopt the idea that "tolerance" is a protected right for all persons from feeling harmed emotionally. This gives rise to terms such as "equity" and "diversity." These liberals would have us place the First Amendment on the chopping block to produce a truly tolerant culture. "Free speech," they tout, "is only free if it does not offend me."

Sadly, the seed bed for such corruption in morality is local college campuses across the nation. Parents, maybe it's time to become a canary to your family by saying to your graduating high school senior, "If you want mom and dad to fund it, you will go to a college that teaches rather than indoctrinates."

Furthermore, it may be time to assist our children to select tracks of education that prepare them with marketable skills when/if they finally graduate.

Next generation leaders are being indoctrinated not educated. And, there is a reason for it. Depraved thinking produces depraved living. In his book, *The Beauty of Intolerance,* philosopher Josh McDowell provides incredible insight as to how cultural tolerance fails us.

Failure 1: Cultural tolerance promises complete moral freedom, but chains us.

Our "anything goes" culture is filled with the allure of promises that are as hollow as a dead log. Remember, a twenty-year old man or woman knows what a twenty-year-old knows—not much. This promise of freedom from morals becomes a trap and a prison.

Failure 2: Cultural tolerance trains us to react to life from a fluid standard of our subjective emotions and personal life experiences.

The sand will always be shifting. That means this generation will live day-by-day based on feelings. If a problem arises, they declare, "It's not my issue." When there is a call to devotion in relationships, they will defend walking away from any relationship that demands commitment in the long term.

Sinking sand. Jesus talked about that unstable, failing foundation describing a fellow who built his house on shifting sands. When turbulent times came, the house fell. Like that house, a life built on shifting sands of cultural tolerance will not be able to stand the tests of life.

Failure 3: Cultural tolerance uses shame to control us—while proving its own intolerance.

How often the terms *hypocrite, judgmental, bigot,* or *racist* become the default setting of this depraved culture! It seems when one has no definitive argument, these cultural would-be bullies resort to calling names. Attributing to others their own biases.

Our culture is as gullible as sheep. Instead of thinking for ourselves, we mindlessly adopt multiple pools of ignorance. For proof, just watch some of the "person-on-the-street" interviews. They are meant to be funny. They are sad. There's no fun in their ignorance.

No Surrender

We do not have to surrender time-honored and proven standards of living to a culture in free fall. We are however, commanded to demonstrate a self-sacrificial kind of love without compromise.

Committed Christians are to love others, to pray for them. But we are not called to accept their toxic mindset. Like Paul challenging the philosophers of Athens on Mars Hill (Acts 17:16-34), we are to challenge the corrupt, twisted thinking of our culture.

A nation that turns away is given over to a reprobate mind. However, just as a remnant endured turbulent times in Israel's history, a remnant survives in our culture and is preparing to speak out.

Our culture did not arrive at this current destination by accident. The calamities we face were not the result of a tsunami. They are the result of unrelenting generational pressure and deception. The recovery will demand unrelenting generational pressure and truth.

Canaries in this cultural free-fall are needed more than ever. Arise!

A Step to take now:

Read President Eisenhower's Farewell Address. Find it at
https://www.archives.gov/milestone-documents.

Chapter Nine
Wake Up to Woke!

"Stay woke."

A watchword for black Americans rooted in the 1930s, *Woke* implies social activism, nationalism, and collectivism. It suggests rage, passion, resistance, and action. It seeks to draw lines against what these activists believe to be unacceptable. This century-old movement was a call to awaken to racial prejudice and discrimination. Often the parting line between friends and activists was, "Stay woke."

It found fuller expression in the civil rights movements of the 60s. And in the more radical movements of the 1970's.

Thomas Sowell reflected on this social undercurrent in an interview he did in 1995. At that time, he was 65 years old. Much of the evaluation he shared was due to his personal experience. He had lived through Jim Crow. He had experienced the civil rights movement. He had walked the halls of academia at Harvard, Columbia, University of Chicago, University of California, and Stanford. He speaks from a lifetime of academic and lived experience. Here's what he said about the caldron that created "woke."

(Sowell) Woke is "a vision that the problems that we see in the world are due to the fact that other people are just not as bright or as compassionate as they (the woke) are. And that there are all these solutions out there waiting to be discovered—and they have them. These solutions will be imposed upon the rest of us by the power of government through taxation or in other ways. What's really crucial about it is that their passion is so much greater than the passion on the other side."

(Interviewer) "Who is the *they*?"

(Sowell) "The media elite, the academic elite, the political elite. And the reason we can talk about their vision (even though they obviously vary in their opinions) is that the basic set of underlying assumptions about the world are very similar. And because these assumptions are the prevailing assumptions, the need to find evidence for them or to offer proof is much less." (Think Tank with Ben Wattenberg, S1 E63, Original air date: October 12, 1995)

Catch what Sowell said about evidence: because the assumptions are broadly shared, less evidence of their veracity is required. Statements of opinion based on assumption can be made and accepted as fact without any underlying empirical data.

Case in point—Black Lives Matter.

Woke Resistance heightened in 2013 after the shooting of 17-year-old Trayvon Martin by George Zimmerman. For instance, Black Lives Matter (the movement, not the scam) hit the streets after the acquittal of Zimmerman. Black Lives Matter adamantly asserted that an epidemic of black men being killed by law enforcement blanketed America. But do the facts support that assertion?

As of the June 22, 2020 update, the Washington Post's database of fatal police shootings showed 14 unarmed black victims and 25 unarmed white victims for the full year of 2019. The data base of nation-wide incidents has been kept since 2015. Of the 7,300 black homicides, these 14 fatal shootings represent .0019% of the black homicides in America. An epidemic rages. But it is not from law enforcement.

This is just one instance that points to the reality of what Sowell stated. Assertions in the woke movement can be made without any

168

underlying data to support them. Whole communities rally around such assertions, thus, splintering the culture.

Woke, however, has morphed into an awareness of additional "perceived wrongs" in our culture. It has taken on a much larger definition and expression.

You don't know what woke means?

"Here's what it means...," said Vivek Ramaswamy to the interviewer. He ought to know. He wrote the book on Woke—quite literally. His book, *Woke, Inc.: Inside Corporate America's Social Justice Scam*, takes aim at what he calls, "the defining scam of our century." Here's his explanation of woke.

"I'm going to define it in neutral terms that nobody can deny okay. Being woke refers to waking up to *invisible, alleged, societal injustices based on genetically inherited attributes: race, sex, and sexual orientation. And further, it creates a hierarchy based on these genetic attributes to say that you're either an oppressor or you're a member of an oppressed class.* Which creates these invisible relationships that creates a social hierarchy.

"And what they say is we need to turn that social hierarchy upside down or at least even it out by using any means necessary—not just through government but even through the private sector; even through our schools; and even through our economy itself including the use of quota systems based on race, gender, and sexual orientation to correct for those alleged societal injustices. That is what it means to be woke. That is what the woke movement is all about."

Woke culture has made victims of all of us.

Woke has given an illegitimate birth to "Cancel Culture." The influence of this mob mentality movement stretches from businesses and banks to baseball and soda water. Woke touches everything in America at this time.

Certain members of this mob have assumed a license has been

169

issued allowing them to remove any part of this culture that appears to oppress or offend them. Their purpose is to divide our culture at every turn. And the people pushing this have been very successful.

Like splitting a round of a log, the pieces are split into smaller and smaller pieces. What began as a single whole has now been split into kindling. When starting a fire, you don't begin with the log. You begin with the smaller pieces. More surface, more air— and soon, you can burn down a whole forest.

America has been split and it is burning down. How many ways have we been split, fragmented? Here are a few. And know at the outset, we cannot deal with all of these. These are just representative of the woke blight afflicting America today.

Philosophically

The minority voice of "Cancel Culture" has a value system that is diametrically opposite to the silent majority of American culture. Where most proclaim freedom, "Cancel Culture" touts tyranny. Law and order is removed by idiocy that defunded police. As a result, rampant crime, drugs, and sex trafficking are contaminating our culture.

Dr. Phil might say, "How's that working for you?" Just ask citizens living in the West Coast cities of San Francisco, Portland, and Seattle who are enduring the effects of "Cancel Culture." Images of charred homes, businesses, and government buildings are etched in the conscience of caring and concerned Americans.

Politically

A kissing cousin to "Cancel Culture" is "Black Lives Matter." Careful, objective evaluation of this organization is eye-opening indeed. Be certain, BLM is a Marxist political movement with an agenda to reshape the entire world.

It proclaims that all black Americans should receive a guaranteed minimum income, free healthcare, schooling, food, real estate, gender reassignment surgery, and abortion on demand. It would close the jails, setting violent criminals loose on our culture.

This is socialism! Travel to any country where socialism exists. You will discover a nation of "have's and have not's." High taxation will force businesses to close. The value of currency is worthless. Remember Prime Minister Margret Thatcher's view on socialism when she said:

The problem with socialism is that you eventually run out of other people's money."

While government hands out cash by the wheelbarrow loads, it's important to know that someone still must foot the bill.

ANTIFA is also linked to this misguided idiocy. Primarily a Caucasian movement, ANTIFA is saturated with a generation of lazy, unemployed, violent, and lawless followers. This group of radicals will never build anything. They only know how to destroy and disrupt.

Economically

It boggles the mind how corporate executives cower to Cancel Culture. It is either a failed attempt to broaden market demand of their product or fear that Cancel Culture will boycott them. These executives should memorize, "Go Woke, Go Broke!" What reasonably intelligent person would sacrifice the whole pie for a sliver?

[And while we address in this chapter facets of this extended *woke* amalgamation, this is all of a piece.

Corporations structure their boards, alter their products, make investments, contribute to the right causes driven by their ESG (Environmental, Social, and Governance) Score. This arbitrary score is used to screen investments that potential investors (individual or corporate) might make. The score is based on corporate policies and is promoted to encourage companies to act "responsibly."

When trying to discover who establishes a company's ESG Score, you discover not government agencies, not independent nonprofit citizen groups, but independently owned businesses. For instance, one such entity is MSCI—that's all you get, just initials. But on their website in the small print, this is what you discover: *MSCI ESG Research LLC. is a Registered Investment Adviser under the Investment Adviser Act of 1940. MSCI ESG Research is an independent provider of ESG data, reports and ratings based on published methodologies and available to clients on a subscription basis.*

There is the scam. Someone had an idea of how to capitalize on the wokeness of current culture. And they are not the only group doing this—Sustainalytics, Gartner, Forrester Research, even the venerable Ernst & Young—are all providing advice to companies on how to raise and secure their ESG scores. If there is a pile of cash on the table, someone is figuring out how to get their share of it. And the rest of us are paying the price for their greed.

Whether the compliant companies advised by these ESG mongers actually believe in this religion or whether they are just virtue signaling, is uncertain. But banks and investors are now taking these ESG scores into account. So you either play the game or you go home empty handed.

And behind all of this is the equity agenda...that we will address in a bit. And just one more aside—if everyone was so concerned about the environment and sustainability, why is nuclear energy always excluded from the discussion? Maybe another agenda is driving all of this hysteria.]

Sorry for the detour. Now back to our topic…

Cancel Culture forced itself on Major League Baseball's edition of the 2021 All Star Game that was scheduled to be played in Atlanta, Georgia. Some officials were pressured to move the summer classic due in part to an election reform bill signed into law that opponents believed "disproportionally disenfranchises people of color." That decision cost Atlanta vendors more than 50 million dollars.

Companies including YouTube, GoDaddy, Amazon, Etsy,

Salesforce, Bank of America, Go Fund Me, and J. P. Morgan continue to roll the economic dice for fear of reprisal from these misguided activists. Ask Anheuser-Busch and Target how going woke has worked out for them. People are fed up with having woke values force-fed to us.

Educationally

One goal of the "Cancel Culture" is to redefine the American experiment from one firmly entrenched in liberty to a culture that finds its roots in slavery. A creation of Nikole Hannah-Jones, the school curriculum, *The 1619 Project*, is a biased, brazen lie. Historians across the board have pointed out its errors. But that has not stopped it from being taught in schools across the nation.

Why is that important? Teaching such material will create a generation of disenfranchised citizens who (especially if you are Caucasian) will be expected to apologize for breathing. Lost in this deceitful curriculum will be a devotion to America and her rich history. Forget history and forget a nation!

This also brings into question why our public schools have become stations of indoctrination rather than education. Whatever happened to "reading, writing, and arithmetic?"

Our culture is allowing the young minds of our children to be systematically indoctrinated rather than being instructed. And because of this, America is losing its edge in math and science. Depending on which survey you read, the United States now ranks behind China and Russia in science. In fact, the Program for International Student Assessment, administered by the Organization for Economic Cooperation and Development (OECD) tests 15-year-old students around the world. The U.S. placed 11th out of 79 countries in science when the test was last administered in 2018. It did much worse in math, ranking 30th.

This generation of students is being pressured to conform to philosophical beliefs and goals by the twisted thinking of leading public educators. When these "educators" use phrases but parents do not know what they mean, that is by design. Our schools are becoming centers for ideological activism rather than teaching fundamentals necessary in equipping students for life.

In 2023, 750 billion dollars will be spent on a public education system that is guilty of "dumbing down" our children. For example, cursive writing is too difficult to perfect, so these computer savvy children may only be exposed to print lettering. Math exams are considered biased to some in the culture while others have not been exposed to the same building blocks of higher math demands. They believe these exams must not be continued. Recent results of year-end math scores in Tennessee show that less than 40% passed math and approximately 30% could not complete the third grade English proficiency exam. Most likely, this is a trend across the nation.

A 750 billion dollar educational investment does not produce the expected outcomes of our citizens. Sounds like a poor investment. The returns are disappointing at best. Imagine how public education would improve were it turned over to the private sector.

Antiracism

Everyone should be opposed to racism. However, "antiracism" is an Orwellian phrase that means exactly the opposite of how it sounds. "Antiracists" agree that society, in every facet, is racist and the remedy is to welcome sweeping new forms of racial discrimination.

Such rhetoric is destructive to our schools and communities. Its goal is to separate people and instill guilt, shame, and resentment toward other groups. "Good people" and "bad people" are being redefined for our children. Good people adopt antiracial demands while bad people reject them.

Equity

What was once understood as fairness or justice, now refers to outcomes. That means opportunity and outcomes produce the same results.

Quotas are an example. Our universities regularly block admission to specific ethnic groups of highly qualified students to reduce the size of those people groups on campuses. Academic merit is sacrificed on the altar of equity's lower standards.

The Supreme Court has just (as of June 29, 2023) announced their ruling that struck down affirmative action policies at colleges, ruling that race-conscious admissions policies at Harvard University and the University of North Carolina are unlawful. "The student must be treated based on his or her experiences as an individual—not on the basis of race," Chief Justice John Roberts wrote in the majority opinion. "Many universities have for too long done just the opposite. And in doing so, they have concluded, wrongly, that the touchstone of an individual's identity is not challenges bested, skills built, or lessons learned but the color of their skin."

What did Martin Luther King, Jr. say in the shadow of the statue of Abraham Lincoln on a sweltering August 28, 1963? He said that he had a dream: "I have a dream that my four little children will one day live in a nation where they will not be judged by the color of their skin but by the content of their character." This ruling is in keeping with that dream.

If America is to advance, it must be a meritocracy. We require equality of opportunity. What a person does with that opportunity is up to them. Equity, however, puts the thumb on the scale. Equity focuses on equality of outcomes. Equity underline forces equality of outcomes. Equity is a way for our nation to spiral continually downward.

Critical Race Theory

This academic philosophy promotes division in our culture. It has been craftily injected into our societal thinking, hidden in plain view, for decades.

"Diversity Training," "Black Studies," and "Reconstructive Curriculum" all have the same inherent goal…to divide the American people. A nation united cannot be enslaved. But a nation divided will not be able to stand. At the heart of CRT is continual indoctrination of racial identity and division as well as LGBTQ+ agendas, gender confusion, and a comprehensive sex education curriculum that promotes pornographic and sexual content to children as young as kindergarten.

Like acid on skin, the foundational element of CRT destroys our culture by accusing our society of systemic, structural racism. It promotes radical, destructive changes because if everything is racist, then everything must be dismantled.

Social Justice

In contemporary politics, social science, and political philosophy, social justice focuses on fair treatment and equitable status of all individuals and social groups within a state or society. The term refers to social, political, and economic institutions, laws, or policies that individually and collectively afford such fairness and equity. The appellation is commonly applied to movements that seek fairness, equity, inclusion, self-determination, or other goals for currently or historically oppressed, exploited, or marginalized populations.

The purpose of this terminology is to make radical political views sound non-political and honest. Disagreeing with this thinking places the burden of proof on those who do not agree with the terminology or maybe the goals and methodologies. This term is loaded like the old question, "Have you stopped beating your wife?" But behind this innocent sounding term is the hidden agenda of dividing our nation.

Micro-aggression

This politically active terminology describes how everyone is a "victim." It is creating generations of children who are emotionally fragile and who think of themselves as being either oppressors or victims.

Those interacting with the sensitive, everyone-gets-a-trophy crowd never knows where the trip wires are. We do not know what will set someone off. This puts a damper on any social exchange— at work, at school, a gathering with friends, even at the grocery store. Persons who have been accused of committing a micro-aggression will often find themselves self-editing their conversations and actions with others.

One man said recently that he is finding it more secure to limit his interaction with others. He has grown cautious because he never knows what conflict he will set off simply by making a comment or having a conversation. Think how that affects a society.

Implicit Association

Although you might not be familiar with the term, you might have been accused of suffering from implicit association. (And you thought the inoculation would have prevented this.) This has to do with biased evaluations or stereotypes one holds. It usually refers to an individual's hidden or subconscious biases. For example, a person might believe that men and women are equally good at math and arts but might be faster to associate math with men and arts with women rather than the other way around.

Even stereotypical phrases like "white men can't jump" indicate implicit association. Or, "Asians are all good at math."

If something is implicit, it is not directly stated. You can suffer from this and not even know it. In most instances, you don't. But in the current environment, one finds that the self-monitoring switch is always in the "on" position. But if at dinner, you give the check to your Asian friend to figure the tip, you might be suffering from implicit association.

White Fragility

At the center of Critical Race Theory is the belief that "all white people are racist, whether they think so or not." When a white person defends against or is upset when being accused of "white privilege," or rejects CRT, such persons are considered "fragile."

These people are described as "emotional, weak, and unwilling to accept the truth" by those who espouse CRT.

Critical Race Theory is described as a cross-disciplinary examination by social and civil-rights scholars and activists of how laws, social and political movements, and media shape and are shaped by social conceptions of race and ethnicity. Sociologists use it to explain social, political, legal structures, and power distribution by focusing on the concept of race and experiences of racism.

Rather than objective, empirical data, CRT often relies on anecdotal and subjective experiences. Key to CRT is intersectionality—the way in which different forms of inequality and identity are affected by interconnections of race, class, gender, and disability. Many facets of grievance are brought under the umbrella of CRT. Proponents are often part of the race grievance industry.

CRT proponents view racism and disparate racial outcomes as the result of complex, changing, and often subtle social and institutional dynamics. The term bandied about is **_systemic_**. Yet, systemic racism is rare or non-existent. When asked to point to evidence of systemic racism, often the sound of crickets is heard.

CRT advocates argue that the social and legal construction of race advances the interests of white people at the expense of people of color. They believe that the concept of U.S. law as neutral only promotes a racially unjust social order in which laws are racially discriminatory.

In the aftermath of the 1960s and 1970s civil rights legislation, colleges and law schools began presenting theories on class, economic structure, and the law to examine the role of U.S. law in perpetuating racism. Those discussions and courses have now been brought into primary and secondary schools across the nation as Critical Race Theory.

Efforts have been made to hide this instruction from parents. However, one of the side effects of Covid-19 was that parents were able to see and hear the instruction being promulgated upon their children. Alarmed parents began arising to stand against this indoctrination. Conservative lawmakers, along with these parents, have joined the fray to ban or restrict the instruction of CRT in our schools.

This ideology has even infected our military ranks. Structures that depend on solidarity and unit cohesion have been assaulted by the very leaders at the top of the military command. The essential cohesion necessary in the military has been shattered.

Opponents of CRT hold that it is false, anti-American, villainizes white people, promotes radical leftism, and indoctrinates children.

Medically

The Bible is clear. The Creator made man and woman. It does not take a rocket scientist to figure that out! However, the twisted view of sexuality is entering the medical field. Life altering surgery to our children will haunt our culture in the future. Furthermore, should surgeons who perform this procedure be held accountable for medical malpractice?

Racially

Black Lives Matter is inherently racist. Why? Because ALL LIVES MATTER. Each of us is marvelously and wondrously made in God's image. If Black Lives Matter, then why has this organization not marched in the streets of one of the deadliest cities in America— Chicago? And what about Washington D. C.? When will BLM address the black-on-black crime racing through our culture? The 7,300 black homicide victims a year call out for someone to stand and demand such insanity and inhumanity end.

If Black Lives really Matter, why is this epidemic not addressed? Why is it only those victims of the rare instance of a black person being killed by law enforcement that is highlighted?

And it is rare that an unarmed black man is killed in a confrontation with the police. How rare? Recall the stats mentioned earlier that in 2019 only 14 such instances occurred. Do the math. In the typical year that means that those incidents comprise .0019% of the homicides. Hardly epidemic. And that is not to downplay these deaths. But it is to highlight all the other wasted lives. Because all lives matter, not just those that play on heightened emotions to achieve divisive objectives.

BLM is more than white words on black t-shirts. It's more than a hashtag. It is a radical movement calling for racial equity, criminal justice reform, and police accountability. It exploded on the culture in the aftermath of the Zimmerman's acquittal. In the violence of the "Summer of Love" of 2020, the money rolled in to the Black Lives Matter Global Network Foundation (the private organization not the larger social movement) to the tune of 90 million dollars.

Corporations and wealthy individuals threw cash at the organization. Whether it was out of genuine support or just virtue signaling, we cannot say. But the three "founders" were flush with cash. Currently approximately two-thirds of these funds, some 60 million dollars, remains unaccounted.

Also, it seems this movement is now leaderless. The founders are no longer involved. No one is at the helm. Citizens will remember that co-founder Patrisse Cullors came under fire for purchasing several multi-million-dollar homes at the exact time George Floyd protests were active. Fundraising ethicists are finding how this foundation utilized their monies to be extremely shady. Black Lives Matter Global Network Foundation has a lot of explaining to do.

Historically

These stateside vandals have a goal to eradicate American history from the conscience and memory of our citizenry. The systematic removal of long-standing monuments weakens our consciousness of history—including its darker side. The iconic monuments of George Washington, Robert E. Lee, Teddy Roosevelt, Abraham Lincoln, and Christopher Columbus (among others) have been targets of radicals who seek to wipe history from the next generation. All of our history must be preserved—the good, the bad, and the ugly. Without the context of history, we will only live to repeat the mistakes of the past.

As this book is being written, our country is remembering our fallen military heroes who gave the ultimate sacrifice for our freedoms. One of those founding freedoms is the right of free speech. That includes the nonsense that is spewed from radicals hiding behind movements like Cancel Culture, Black Lives Matter, and Woke. But this also means that the freedom of speech of conservative, patriotic Americans is also protected.

Oppressed and Oppressors

All elements of the Woke movement can be grouped under the banner of neo-Marxism. What used to be classic liberalism in society has morphed into a radical Marxism. Especially has this been espoused and propagated on college campuses. Just look at what is happening around the world to see who is participating. A common source is to be found. Colleges now serve as indoctrination centers.

Why did 1960s radicals like those from the Weather Underground become college professors? (You might not be familiar with this radical group. The group's stated political goal was to create a revolutionary party to overthrow the United States government. The FBI at that time described the group as a domestic terrorist group.)

Why become college professors? They knew that if they could influence and shape impressionable students, they could influence the future. It took nearly fifty years, but that future has arrived.

How effective have they been? The structures of government and society have been so influenced that today parents attending school board meetings, traditional Catholics praying the rosary and worshipping through the Latin mass, and America-loving conservative Christians have been pronounced domestic terrorists. Isaiah had it right. Everything has been turned on its head—right is wrong, wrong is right; light is dark and dark is light (Is. 5:20).

The key wedge this movement uses to divide people, governments, and societies is *the wedge of oppressed and oppressors.*

In every element of our culture this wedge is being used to pit one group against another. One ethnic group against another, women against men, poor against rich, Black against White, secular against religious. No longer cohesive, the culture will fail. As Jesus stated, *a kingdom divided against itself cannot stand.*

The Sanctity of Life and Liberty

God, the Giver of life, values all lives. The Psalmist recognized the hand of God in his creation:

For you formed my inward parts; you knitted me together in my mother's womb. I praise you, for I am fearfully and wonderfully made. Wonderful are your works; my soul knows it very well.
(Psalm 139:13-14)

The psalmist knew that he mattered because God had formed him in his mother's womb. He marveled at his Creator.

The principle and the promise of America, from its Declaration to its Constitutional founding, is that all lives matter. All have the rights to life, liberty, and the pursuit of happiness. These rights are inalienable. Their origin is God, not the state.

Calling upon the Laws of Nature and of Nature's God, the signers of the Declaration affirmed:

> We hold these truths to be self-evident, that all men are created equal, that they are endowed by their Creator with certain unalienable Rights, that among these are Life, Liberty and the pursuit of Happiness.—That to secure these rights, Governments are instituted among Men, deriving their just powers from the consent of the governed, —That whenever any Form of Government becomes destructive of these ends, it is the Right of the People to alter or to abolish it, and to institute new Government, laying its foundation on such principles and organizing its powers in such form, as to them shall seem most

likely to effect their Safety and Happiness. Prudence, indeed, will dictate that Governments long established should not be changed for light and transient causes; and accordingly all experience hath shewn, that mankind are more disposed to suffer, while evils are sufferable, than to right themselves by abolishing the forms to which they are accustomed. But when a long train of abuses and usurpations, pursuing invariably the same Object evinces a design to reduce them under absolute Despotism, it is their right, it is their duty, to throw off such Government, and to provide new Guards for their future security.

The Framers opened the Constitution with these words:

We the People of the United States, in Order to form a more perfect Union, establish Justice, insure domestic Tranquility, provide for the common defence (sic), promote the general Welfare, and secure the Blessings of Liberty to ourselves and our Posterity, do ordain and establish this Constitution for the United States of America.

In these foundational documents, the ideals of our country were delineated. When these ideals are diminished and abandoned, the fabric of the nation is weakened. Eventually, the fabric gives way. Tatters and rags result. It seems that the fabric of America is fraying.

Our government is to be the steward, the caretaker of our liberties. One key element of that stewardship is that our laws are to be administered justly without regard of person. Then, and only then, will the blessing of God be upon the nation. Amos, Micah, and Isaiah all stated this truth—without justice, the woe of God will be upon us. Blessings will be missed. Micah said it succinctly—*He has told you, O man, what is good; and what does the LORD require of you but to do justice, and to love kindness, and to walk humbly with your God (6:8)?*

All the issues touched upon in this chapter tear at the fabric of America. The cords that bind us together are fraying.

Are we to be silent? Remember the popular phrase warning against complacency: "The only thing necessary for the triumph of evil is for good people to do nothing."

The eighteenth-century Irish philosopher and statesman Edmund Burke stated a similar sentiment in this way: "When bad men combine, the good must associate; else they will fall, one by one, an unpitied sacrifice in a contemptible struggle."

And the British philosopher, John Stuart Mill stated: "Bad men need nothing more to compass their ends, than that good men should look on and do nothing."

What are these all saying? *Now is the time to speak. Now is the time to act.* Could one canary be found as a sentinel to this culture in crisis? Maybe you are feeling a divine tap on your shoulder? If so, respond like Isaiah, *"Here I am. Send me."*

Steps to take now:

Action # 1: Become an advocate for child protective services in your community.

Action # 2: Be aware of the Woke agenda in your community. When you see it, stand against it. Challenge the thinking of Woke with someone who has been misguided because of it.

Action # 3: Express your convictions about Woke to any retailer in your community who supports it.

Action # 4: Be willing to stand against any political, religious, medical, or educational leaders and institutions that abuse power and position in the name of LGBTQ+.

Action # 5: Establish a time each day to read Ezekiel 16:48-50 and Nehemiah 1. These two passages can be used to focus on the plight of America and move us to pray for personal and national repentance.

Chapter Ten
"There's Nothing New Under the Sun"

The gruesome scene was the Alfred P. Murray Federal Building located in Oklahoma City, Oklahoma. Today, the bombing stands as the deadliest act of domestic terrorism in American history.

That day 168 precious souls, including 19 children were murdered at the hands of Timothy James McVeigh. The blast from a homemade bomb also injured 680 people and destroyed one third of the federal building.

A sergeant in the United States Army, McVeigh was a decorated Gulf War veteran receiving an Army Service Ribbon, the Kuwaiti Liberation Medal, as well as a Bronze Star. He was the victim of school bullying and fantasized of ways to execute plans to retaliate against those who abused him. During his high school years, McVeigh became more deeply reserved and so quiet that his senior classmates voted McVeigh as "most talkative" as a joke because he rarely spoke.

The emotional scars left in his life were deep. His hatred for "bullying" intensified when he witnessed the unnecessary carnage by the federal government's actions against David Koresh and his followers who were barricaded in their Waco, Texas compound. His demented response was to attack the federal government. On April 19, 1995, his plans were executed.

It is believed that Michael Fortier, a close friend to McVeigh, was one of two people who knew the diabolical plans to destroy the federal building. Fortier remained silent about the bombing in hopes he could parlay his knowledge into a fortune. He was convicted of being an accomplice to this crime and sentenced to prison for 12 years but was released after serving 10 of those years.

Imagine if only Michael Fortier had been a faithful sentinel who warned authorities of this dastardly crime beforehand! His silence contributed to the bombing in Oklahoma City and the blood of 168 people remains on his hands.

Artificial Intelligence

Today, a moral and ethical bomb is poised to detonate on unsuspecting people throughout our nation. For many Artificial Intelligence (AI) might not be on their radar. However, when we look just over the horizon, rising like a bomb-laden ship that is revealed out of the blind of the earth's curvature as it sails toward us, is Artificial Intelligence. When that ship explodes, there will be societal carnage and uncalculated collateral damage to our culture. This on-coming threat scares even its creators.

It is not necessary that ethicists and moralists have a commanding understanding of the technology used in creating an Artificial Intelligence. The intention of this book is that present-day sentinels engage to "protect" without being emersed in the "tech." A sentinel warns of potential hazards and impending perils threatening those he is commissioned to serve.

In the spring of 2023, Dr Geoffrey Hinton, the man who is often referred to as the "godfather of AI," quit his decade-long job with Google. He resigned in order to address concerns about Artificial Intelligence. He did so out of an ethical position of not wanting to hurt or be in conflict with his employer.

Dr. Hinton's concerns range from misinformation, manipulation, potential harm to job markets, to even the existential risk to humanity. He has described these threats as "quite scary." And especially, if the technology winds up in the hands of bad actors on the world's stage. If the godfather of AI is concerned, maybe the rest of us have the right to be alarmed as well.

Positive Aspects of Artificial Intelligence

Arguments for how Artificial Intelligence will assist our culture abound. Aeronautics might be placing a highly intelligent machine in the capsule of a space craft. Maybe long journeys to distant planets such as Mars become a safer reality sooner. It could be that Artificial Intelligence is among the necessary machines to help mankind as we inhabit the moon. It has been said that science fiction writers are the prophets of our future. Think about the portrayals of AI in books and films such as Hal in *2001: A Space Odyssey*, the droids like r2d2 of *Star Wars*, or TARS in *Interstellar*. These are all machines that helped the humans achieve their missions—or not in the case of Hal.

The field of medicine might also benefit from Artificial Intelligence. Imagine having a source with the collective medical wisdom to address complicated medical diagnoses. Capable of searching all the medical journals and research available in a matter of moments to make a diagnosis, suggest treatment, or develop a cure.

Artificial Intelligence could be that source. Just think how patient care escalates when a nationwide need for unfilled nursing positions is addressed with Artificial Intelligence. Could there be discoveries for cures of cancer, Parkinson's, dementia, arthritis, glaucoma, or any other malady of people just around the corner?

The marketplace will also feel positive effects from Artificial Intelligence. It is believed that one day soon travelers will drive up to the windows of fast-food establishments for service. Then, Artificial Intelligence will receive food orders, prepare the food, deliver it to the customer, and complete financial steps for that order. What a thought—AI might return "fast" to fast-food!

It is conceivable that AI can support any field of expertise by becoming an answer to nagging questions of that industry. Artificial

Intelligence is on track to be very powerful. Caution is needed. Fire can be helpful if it is contained. Ice is useful in various ways. Water is essential for our very existence. However, like fire, ice, and water, this technology can be abused. Fire can burn us. Ice can freeze us. Flooding can destroy property, possessions, and people.

Negative Aspects of Artificial Intelligence

Orville and Wilber Wright were inventors of the airplane. When planes were invented, so were "plane crashes." Is our culture boarding a doomed technological flight? Several issues point to immediate dangers of an unhinged and unvetted AI technology. When one drills down into concerns about Artificial Intelligence several issues arise.

Issue # 1: How is Artificial Intelligence Defined?

Remember, black words on white paper or a computer screen mean something. Webster defines "artificial" as, "not genuine, made by man, not found in nature." Related words are sham, substitute, fictitious, simulated, and fake. The inventors of AI are stirring up a dish that could be detrimental to our culture. Like a witch's brew meant to control or destroy, AI is in the pot. A closer examination of the terms "Artificial Intelligence" categorizes it as an oxy-moron.

It seems inventors of AI have huge intellectual blind spots. Or maybe there is a well-planned agenda hidden deeply within the technology. Like nailing Jello® to a wall, defining AI encompasses such broad applications that the inventors of this machine process can hide behind ideation, thoughts, and opinions that are simply unverifiable. It is difficult to get a definition that sticks. AI is a term used to describe machines performing human-like cognitive processes such as learning, understanding, reasoning, and interacting.

Our culture is embracing incipient Artificial Intelligence. Smart -phones provide a smart assistance called Siri®, to perform a variety of tasks for users. Tesla® cars are connected so that information any one car learns is shared across the entire fleet. Our phones are queued to recognize our faces for security. We play games that are driven by AI. Our farms use AI for weed identification and eradication. More and more our lives are being influenced daily by AI.

A definition of AI? The Organization for Economic Cooperation and Development (OECD) is a forum comprised of 37 democracies with market-based economies who collaborate to develop policy standards that promote sustainable economic growth. OECD has stated, "However, our research shows there is no definable terminology to hang one's hat upon that adequately describes the power and problems of AI. Certainly, the display of this revolutionary and brilliant technology affirms that mankind (including these inventors) has always been and will always be finite thinkers."

That means inventors of AI do not have infinite knowledge nor have the capacity to know the full impact of AI. Simply put, they don't know what they don't know about the power of this machine. In the words of Mark Twain,

"We are all ignorant, just about different things."

The inventors of AI have levels of brilliance few others can claim. However, it should be remembered that the more we know, the more we know we ought to know. One glaring concern is not what inventors of AI know, but rather, what they do not know.

Before this technology is unleashed on our culture, it would be wise to revisit the end of World War II and recall the devastating effects of nuclear weaponry. The inventors today are no different than those limited thinkers of bygone years. It is a gamble. And the stakes are incredibly high for our culture and that of the world. That is a troubling thought indeed.

Issue # 2: Where Does it Stop?

It is feared a "ready, fire, aim" mindset is deeply imbedded in AI. Such incomplete thinking is irresponsible. Many observers would welcome a strategy that includes placing evaluative tools and measurable standards in the process of creating and launching AI. It is beginning with the end in mind. In short, before embarking on any promising journey this technology advertises, a closer look at the route to its perceived destination is in order. Like certain choices in life, we may get what we want but will we want what we are going to get?

One way to address this issue is by envisioning the end before jumping headlong into the process of creating AI. These visioning exercises are engaged in everything from developing a blueprint for a building or mapping a life path for your future. Everyone from engineers to life coaches know the value of creating in thought exercises the end result that is desired. To enhance the potential of success, evaluation instruments are developed to identify strengths, weaknesses, problems, threats, challenges, and opportunities.

What evaluative measurements have been put in place for Artificial Intelligence? AI is forcing our culture to board ship to an unknown destination. When the boat sails, how will our culture know when it has arrived at AI's promised destination? "Ready, fire, aim" is unacceptable when it comes to this speculative technology.

We are not seeking to be Luddites. The Luddites were members of the textile workers in England during the early 1800s who resisted the incorporation of machinery into the textile industry. We see the benefits AI can bring. But we join the hundreds of AI leaders such as Hinton, Musk, Wozniak, Altman, and others who are expressing concern about the rapid development and deployment of this technology. They have all signed an open letter calling for a pause in the development of AI. They are concerned about the effects of this technology on the world. And these are not Luddites. But they are concerned leaders. If the developers are concerned, maybe we should be as well.

Issue # 3: It's About Control!

Chicken Little incessantly told all her barnyard buddies "the sky is falling" so often that they stopped believing her. Is our cultural sky falling before our eyes? Or is it possible that legitimate concerns arising from thinking people have not been invited to the intellectual party surrounding AI? Connor Leahy is an AI researcher and ethicist. He thinks deeply about the alignment of AI with the values and ethics of our culture. He has said that the local sandwich shop has more regulations than does AI development. Scary.

Like opposite sides of a coin, there are gargantuan opportunities linked to even larger warnings. One clear and present danger relates to our national security. A recent interview with Russian president, Vladimir Putin, should put a chill down the spine of every American. Putin believes that the international race to develop Artificial Intelligence will determine the next world power.

"Artificial Intelligence is the future, not only for Russia, but for all humankind," said Putin. "It comes with colossal opportunities, but also threats that are difficult to predict. Whoever becomes the world leader in this sphere will become the ruler of the world."

The Verge

These chilling words are spoken by a man who has invaded the sovereign country of Ukraine. His ambition included gaining control of territories lost when USSR was dismantled on December 26, 1991. Putin is a dangerous world leader who cannot and must not be trusted. In fact, on March 17, 2023, the International Criminal Court issued an arrest warrant against Putin for war crimes that include "unlawful deportation of population (children) and that of unlawful transfer of population (children) from occupied territories of Ukraine to the Russian Federation."

The twisted and corrupt view of this war criminal toward world domination is highlighted by nearly 370,000 Russian and Ukrainian military deaths since the beginning of his unlawful siege on Ukraine. Only the naive would think that *if* he conquers Ukraine, that he will stop there. Just ask any thinking person living on Russia's border. Putin will not stop on his own. He must be stopped especially when it comes to technological advances of AI.

It smacks of tensions that thrust the world into aeronautical races of the 1960's and the nuclear race in 1980's. Imagine if/when Putin (as a vassal leader, subservient to China's domination) joins the AI race—and wins.

However, like a broken clock is correct twice a day, even wicked leaders who are compulsive liars, get it right sometimes. And Putin got the AI question right. Whoever gets there first will control the world.

The China Card

China joins the United States as a front-runner in developing AI. Remember, China's goal remains to be the dominating force on our culture as well as the rest of the world. Putin has stated that he does not want an AI race to be a winner-take-all scenario, nor does he want to see any one country monopolize the technology—except (secretly believed by himself) for Russia.

When it comes to global control, it is feared that Putin would lead Russia to join with China in this AI arms race. So concerning is the threat AI poses that Elon Musk and 116 other technology leaders have sent a petition to the United Nations that calls for stiff regulations on how AI weapons are developed. It is believed that like the inventing of gun powder more than a 1000 years ago and the creation of atomic weaponry in the 1940's, today's threat will be tantamount to a third revolution in warfare.

A problematic scenario might be on the horizon. Let's suppose that America complies with the stiff regulations on how AI weapons are developed. It might mean that our country falls behind in the race for global dominance behind other nations that refuse compliance—like China. Does anyone in their right mind believe that China (or Russia) is going to comply with ANY regulations sanctioned by an ever-weakening body called the United Nations?

A fine line must be considered here. Yes, every developed nation in the world needs to pump the brakes on this technology until there is consensus on the operational venues of AI. Someone will suggest treaties between nations to agree on the applications of AI. The problem is that treaties are about as helpful as a screen door on a submarine. They are as reliable as a typical weather forecast. Ask any of the indigenous tribal nations how the United States stood by its treaties. (Just to use an inconvenient historical fact.)

Dignitaries might agree face-to-face but it is what goes on when no one is looking that should concern all of us. Remember, we cannot expect transparency when we are not allowed to inspect. Our history with Iranians toward enriching uranium is a preview of the disastrous movie that might be coming soon to a theater near us.

Maybe Chicken Little has something our culture needs to hear.

Issue # 4: How does AI affect business?

Artificial Intelligence is already here. It's real and it's quickening. Kevin Kelly in his book, *The Inevitable: Understanding the 12 Technological Forces That Will Shape Our Future,* stated, "I think the formula for the next 10,000 start-ups is to take something that already exists and add AI to it." Proponents of AI believe small businesses across our country may experience economic growth that otherwise would be absent. Businesses may optimize their operations and enhance customer experience. AI is emerging as a game-changing technology.

Chatbots are becoming increasingly prevalent for their ability to mimic human-like conversations and perform routine tasks. Small business can use Chatbots to deliver prompt and seamless customer service reducing waiting times and cutting staffing costs.

AI assists small businesses in creating and implementing personalized marketing tools. It will be able to send marketing messages, email campaigns, social media ads, and other content that targets a customer's unique needs and interests. We all experience this now. Every time we do a search using Google, our next suggested articles or inquiries are shaped by AI. The screens of your devices evidence AI at work.

AI can be optimized to create content that personalizes marketing for small businesses. It might mean that consumers and companies are able to connect in more meaningful ways. Many proponents of AI-driven marketing solutions might get a competitive advantage over their competitors. It is believed that AI will save businesses time and money. That might jeopardize jobs now filled by humans.

What role will humans have with A.I. *in business?*

This is a key question for many. For we might be those tossed on the "obsolete" pile.

Today, AI is becoming good at many "human" jobs – translating languages, providing customer service, and even diagnosing disease. And the machine is improving quickly. Concerns that AI will replace human workers throughout the economy, say the experts, is not inevitable or even a most likely outcome. These experts see AI as a "tool" that responds to and enhances human involvement.

It is believed that AI will radically alter how work is completed and who is responsible for it. Executives who are using AI to automate processes think that this technology's larger impact will be in complementing and augmenting human capabilities, not replacing them.

But consider how the job market is changing. Simply look at the local burger joint or any of the self-checkout kiosks at your grocery store or any of the businesses you frequent. Those kiosks are machines taking the place of human workers. If we want a job in the world that is forming, we might need to look at jobs that cannot be done by a machine.

Three primary tasks must be performed by humans in dealing with AI. First, these machines *must be trained* to perform specific tasks. Second, certain assigned tasks *are to be explained* especially if the results are counterintuitive or controversial. Third, responsible use of AI is *to be sustained* so as to protect the human operator from risk of losing employment.

A Cautionary Tale

The story of John Henry, the steel driving man from Talcott, WV, informs us here. According to the tall tale of the man who challenged the steam drill of a by-gone era—using two 10-pound hammers, one in each hand, John Henry pounded the drill so fast and so hard that he drilled a 14-foot hole into the rock. The legend says that the steam drill was only able to drill nine feet. John Henry beat the steam drill and later died of exhaustion. (www.nps.gov)

What price must humanity pay in the future toward which our science is pushing us?

Issue # 5: Intellectual Integrity

This is where concerned patriots step up. Wisdom would saturate the conversation surrounding Artificial Intelligence with legitimate questions. For example, educators are bracing for the damaging effects caused by a writing app called, "ChatGPT." The problem with application of Artificial Intelligence in education is that students are allowing AI to write their assigned papers. All a student has to do is type in a prompt and magically an entire essay is created.

Students do not have to invest time or effort if they know how to work this app. Today's students are way ahead of their teachers anyway. They understand the world of computers (with all the offshoots) and take full advantage of their technological abilities.

This becomes an additional burden on educators as they discover ways students use technology such as ChatGPT to cheat. It is difficult for most teachers to identify plagiarism or artificially produced work. Counter websites have been designed to detect if something has been written by AI or a student. Even with ChatGPT, a person can copy an essay back into the generator and ask if the generator wrote it. AI will be honest about it and lay claim to the paper.

What problems are created when using AI in writing school papers?

The disciplines of integrity, honor, and learning the importance of hard work are sacrificed as students allow AI to do their thinking for them. Critical thinking is underdeveloped. Laziness becomes acceptable in a student's education.

Now imagine if doctors, dentists, ministers, lawyers, and others cheated their way through their educational years. What kind of professionals would they become? Think of the chaos created by those people who take short cuts in technological school training. Should these people be given opportunity to obtain a business license? Would a wise person call into their home for any household repairs a plumber, electrician, or HVAC tech that "hotwired" their training?

Issue # 6: Morality—Who determines AI's World View?

Should creators/inventors/programmers/investors be given the opportunity to launch AI on our culture when it seems that no boundaries have been established and, if so, are not in public view?

Another question that must be analyzed to the satisfaction of canary skeptics is answering objections in the realm of morality. A biblical world view creates a biblical morality. Scripture rightly declares, *There is a way that **seems right** to man, but its end is the way of death* (Proverbs 16:25).

Canaries, allow two little words to soak into your thinking about AI and morality. "Seems right" is a sentinel call for sure. Remember, there is nothing new under the sun. Even after God sent twelve sentinels to His people, Judges 17:6 notes— *Everyone did what was right in their own eyes.*

The concept of "morality" and typical American business, science, politics, or technology rarely collide in the same sentence. Oftentimes, morality is a back-burner issue. An out-of-sight, out-of-mind kind of issue. A common saying is fitting here… "garbage in, garbage out!" If we want a moral outcome, then, we need to have a moral input.

Now is the time for canaries to ask pointed questions about AI and morality. Consider a few:

- Who are the creators of AI?

- Is collaboration with other creators of AI welcomed?

- It is assumed that AI might become self-aware. Will AI programmers be properly vetted to protect this from being reality?

- What happens if inventors/programmers have certain political positions that are contrary to the majority of Americans?

- What happens if inventors/programmers are atheistic or agnostic?

- Suppose AI becomes self-aware and its inventors/programmers support Communism or Socialism?

- AI can be turned on but is there a kill switch somewhere in the machine?

- Will AI be antagonistic to or align with the Ten Commandments?

- And there are more questions and concerns...

Wary sentinels might ask additional questions. This is where our First Amendment Right comes into play. AI proponents might also secretly operate without allowing citizens to voice their concerns. Currently, no platform is designed for this kind of dialogue.

Issue # 7: Relational—Not Good to Be Alone

Perversion never takes a day off. A growing trend in the Japanese culture is called "fictosexuality." The term describes those people who are sexually attracted to fictional characters. Companies are racing to develop technology that offers holographic couples.

Akihiko Kondo took another step in his love-life by "getting married" with Hatsune Miku, a virtual singer who has starred in several video games and has even accompanied Lady Gaga on her world tours.

We must wonder what gift Kondo presents his hologram mate during those special occasions?

If it was not so mind-numbingly dumb, Kondo's cry for attention deserves to be showered with pity. Why? He is lonely. Japan has 100 females to every 96 males. The chances are pretty good that that special "female human" would be discovered sometime in the future. Yet, an artificial relationship is sought in a growing number of cases.

Get ready. Fasten your seatbelt because Artificial Intelligence will be landing into all kinds of relationships world-wide. And in some instances, it will be an easier relationship than those in the real world. It will not matter what your appearance is. It will not matter what kind of car you drive. It will not matter if you have a car. It will not matter how much money you have or don't have. It will not matter what scent you use. As a matter of fact, you can smell like a soured, wet dog. It will not matter that you have never seen the inside of a gym. None of this matters in the world of AI relationships. In a world dominated by AI-generated relationships, any person can become anything or anyone they can imagine.

According to the Center for Disease Control, 40% of Americans are obese. Heart disease, stroke, diabetes, osteoarthritis, and certain kinds of cancer are major risks that accompany obesity. Obesity will be on the rise and have no signs of slowing down. Why? Because people have their noses in some hand-held computer game or they choose to text their friend who is sitting across the table from them. When it comes to an active lifestyle, will AI challenge or acquiesce to this computer age?

AI can never address the needs of humanity. It does not have the capacity to care for people. It is a machine. That means social ills that plague our culture such as pornography, alcohol, drugs, and gambling addiction will not receive comfort and consolation from a machine. If anything, the ills of persons and society will only grow.

Need an example? When you feel a bout of loneliness, go sit in your car and ask Siri for comfort. Most likely, her response will be silence. What else should we expect from a machine?

Issue # 8: Theological—the Pursuit of the Divine

Education can be purchased. Wisdom is gift from God. Just ask Solomon. At the beginning of his reign as the king of Israel, God came to Solomon in a dream and offered him anything that Solomon might desire. He asked God for wisdom and knowledge (2 Chron. 1:7-10). God granted him that and all the attendant things that come with it—fame, wealth, success.

Of all the things he could have requested, the King of Israel asked for *wisdom*. His wisdom remains a foundation for any culture that chooses to build upon it.

Theological concerns come with the creation of Artificial Intelligence. MIT professor and researcher, Max Tegmark says we're not in an arms race. We are in a race to our own destruction. The race is to create a god-like AI. This moves us into the realm of theological implications.

The ultimate goal of AI development is Artificial General Intelligence (AGI). This would be a totally sentient super intelligence—the God machine. The original lie is held out to draw us in—*You will be like God* (the Serpent, Genesis 3:5).

One concern revolves around the hope that AI will become "self-aware." Does that mean it's thinking borders on knowing "everything?" Is it likely for AI to become omniscient?

World-wide there have been eight people identified with very high IQs. They are Jacob Barnett, Judit Polgar, Rick Rosner, Evangelos Katsioulis, Sho Yano, Nathan Leopold, Marilyn vos Savant, and Ainan Crawley (whose I.Q. is 263). Just for the record Albert Einstein's IQ was a mere 160. Yet, AI will be superior to any one of these geniuses or all of them combined.

For instance, Artificial Intelligence experts have already discovered this technological marvel has a measurable intelligence quotient that is 40% higher than the average human on trivia. When it comes to SAT questions, AI scores 15% higher than an average college applicant. Some models of AI can recognize and produce speech for more than 1000 languages. It is the Tower of Babel in reverse.

AI will be able to search data bases world-wide in fractions of seconds to find solutions to problems or answers to questions. And the argument can be made—Is that really intelligence? When are those leaps of insight made that truly mark intelligence? Sentience, self-awareness, creativity? These are the Holy Grails of the quest for AGI.

Dr. Hinton helped enable the rise of technologies that were once the stuff of science fiction movies. He pioneered facial recognition plus chatbots like OpenAI's ChatGPT and Google's Bard. When he stepped away from his position at Google, Hinton voiced concerns that the race between Microsoft and Google will push forward the development of AI without appropriate guardrails and regulations in place.

Two alarming concerns are being voiced by this 75-year-old technological canary.

- First, he is concerned about the interaction of powerful new AI systems with human beings. AI is beginning to reason.

- Second, the software needed to become more complex, that akin to the human brain, is being misjudged. Currently, PaLM has complexity that makes the human brain pale in comparison. (PaLM is a parallel large language model that is the basis for breakthrough research in machine learning or Artificial Intelligence. PaLM excels at advanced reasoning tasks, including code and math, classification and question answering, translation and multilingual proficiency, and natural language generation.) It has the capacity to perform reasoning that humans take a lifetime to attain. As AI algorithms expand, they might outstrip human creators within a few years. Hinton, who once believed that breakthrough was 30 to 50 years away, now declares it more likely 5 to 20 years.

When AI leaders like Hinton, Musk, Wozniak, Altman, and others sound the alarm about AI, the rest of us need to be aware of the dangers AI presents. We will lose more and more of our culture, our humanity, as AI develops.

AI is developing a god-like self-awareness. On the surface, this technology seems to be a breakthrough for the ages. However, attempts to become like God are as old as the Bible.

Deception of the First Couple and Cultures

Adam and Eve, the first couple of humanity, stepped beyond divine standards. Their future was sacrificed on the altar of lies that they would assuredly have their eyes opened and would be like God, knowing good and evil.

Interestingly, before this demonic trap was set, Adam and Eve only knew of "good."

A few pages into the Sacred Text beyond the account of the Serpent's lie, a second attempt to become God–like is detailed. The scene of deception was centered in the land of Shinar, which today is believed to be territory located south of the Turkish mountains between the Tigris and Euphrates rivers. According to Genesis 10:8 -12, Nimrod, "a mighty hunter before the Lord," became the ruler of a kingdom called Babel. Yes, the one of tower fame.

"A rose by any other name…" is still a rose. So too is pride. Shade it, redefine it, deny it—it is still pride. Pride assembled people to begin erecting towering buildings called, "ziggurats." These massive structures were erected in ancient Mesopotamia. Today, famous ziggurats stand in Egypt. We know them as the Pyramids.

Nimrod's prideful attempt to reach God failed miserably. Pride remains as the initial cause for cultural failure since time began. When people become prideful, they are capable of believing and

201

doing anything. Like launching headlong into developing technology that is capable of being all-knowing—like God.

Paul warned that pride would be prevalent in days just prior to the coming of the Lord. Look at the list of characteristics people would display. Compare this list to the characteristics being displayed in our current culture:

> *For people will be lovers of self, lovers of money, proud, arrogant, abusive, disobedient to their parents, ungrateful, unholy, heartless, unappeasable, slanderous, without self-control, brutal, not loving good, treacherous, reckless, swollen with conceit, lovers of pleasure rather than lovers of God, having the appearance of godliness, but denying its power* (2 Timothy 3:2-5).

One indicator marking an end-time scenario would be a global culture fixated on "knowledge." They would always learn but never arrive—to omniscience.

Why? Because omniscience is a theological term describing one of the absolute attributes of God. Omniscience is part of a triad of "omni" attributes.

- God is omnipresent – He is ever present.
- God is omnipotent – He is all powerful.
- God is omniscient – He is all knowing.

God has intuitive, simultaneous, and infallible perceptions of Himself and all other beings. We see culture through filters of prejudice. God sees and knows all things accurately. His omniscience means He knows everything. His understanding is infinite.

Isaiah 40:13-14 asks: *Who has directed the Spirit of the Lord, or as His counselor has informed Him? With whom did He consult and who gave Him understanding? And who taught Him in the path of justice and taught Him knowledge and informed Him of the way of understanding?*

Since His knowledge is infinite, the Lord never learns anything. He never forgets anything either. God is omniscient. No man or machine will ever reach His divine knowledge.

Building a machine that could become self-aware with incomparable knowledge on human standards is a contemporary ziggurat. The Tower of Babel symbolizes man's pride in bygone years. Developing Artificial Intelligence embodies man's pridefulness today.

Pride is deadly according to the Scriptures. *Pride goes before destruction, and a haughty spirit before a fall* (Proverbs 16:18).

The personification of Wisdom states: *The fear of the LORD is hatred of evil. Pride and arrogance and the way of evil and perverted speech I hate* (Proverbs 8:13).

Hannah, the mother of Samuel, in her prayer to God realized the truth of God's ultimate power. In His presence, we have no reason for pride and arrogance. Her prayer rings through time to us:

> *"There is none holy like the Lord:*
> *for there is none besides you;*
> *there is no rock like our God.*
> *Talk no more so very proudly,*
> *let not arrogance come from your mouth;*
> *for the Lord is a God of knowledge,*
> *and by him actions are weighed* (1 Sam. 2:2-3).

God hated pride in the past. He introduced various languages so the Tower Project would fail. He will not allow technology to elevate mankind or machines to become like Him.

The heart of the matter is a matter of the heart!

Will we recognize God as rightful Ruler of the universe? Or will we pay the price for pride?

If a canary could talk, it would tell you there is nothing new under the sun.

Steps to take now:

Action # 1: Pray about the idolatry evident in your community. Ask the Lord for deliverance.

Action # 2: Call on your representatives to support legislation that calls for a discontinuation of research and application of Artificial Intelligence until there is verifiable evidence supporting claims that AI cannot turn on humanity.

Action # 3: Contact your local school board and encourage them to hire quality teachers.

Action # 4: Become savvy concerning how the federal government is using AI against the citizenry including you! Discover ways to identify AI in your everyday life.

Chapter Eleven
"Is There Any Hope?"

The Japanese have a process they call "The Kaizen Effect." This is a process for improvement of products, work, any variety of activities and actions. In particular the mindset touches manufacturing and service industries throughout the culture. The focus is ***incremental improvement***. Small moves. We could achieve a 1,000% improvement in a couple of ways. One is to find a single action that can yield 1,000% improvement. The other is to find a 1,000 actions that can each yield a 1% improvement. Which is more feasible?

Auto manufacturing benefits from the Kaizen Effect by encouraging creative thinking in the ranks of their labor force. These employees are challenged to contribute potential ideas for *daily changes* to automobiles. Such changes equal a mere ¼ of 1%. Over a 240 workday calendar, a 24% change will occur with that product. Four years later those Japanese automobiles have been completely changed.

Changes in a culture are taken in incremental steps too. Like a hunting lion, these movements are subtle, almost imperceivable and unrecognizable. Granted some changes are beneficial to people; others are detrimental. The degenerating morality of our country illustrates a devious and well-planned agenda by those who are seeking *effective* and *affective* change. Whereas the domain of effective change is practical, affective change addresses "feelings." Both can be dominated by wickedness and perversion.

Buttonholes and Beer

Sometimes it just happens. And it likely happens to everyone. Maybe it's happened to you. Have you ever been dressing with a blouse, shirt, or vest and get buttonholes and buttons misaligned? You know something is not right. You *feel* it. One look in a mirror and you can see the problem. Aligning buttons and buttonholes is fundamentally simple. However, sometimes even simple things can get out of sorts.

That is occurring in our culture too. Something is not right about us. We feel it. If we look carefully, we can see it. Unless you have been living on the moon, shock waves are being felt by American corporations that promote lifestyles that simply do not square with the common man.

Anheuser-Busch, the fourth bestselling brand of beer, brews Bud Light. Since April 1, 2023, the market value has dropped $27 billion (that's with a B) based on conversion of U. S. dollars. Why such a financial tumble? (New York Post, June 2, 2023)

April 1, 2023 is when Dylan Mulvaney, a TikTok influencer, who happens to also be a transgender woman, pitched the Bud Light brand during the NCAA March Madness basketball tournament. Backlash to this advertising move was swift and pointed as beer lovers completely turned away from Bud Light and chose other brands. Conservative consumers called for a boycott of the product. Within a month, Bud Light sales dropped by 26%. As of this writing, sales have declined for 17 straight weeks. Economists predict a subset of American consumers will not drink Bud Light for the foreseeable future. Many consumers have left permanently.

By the way, during this same time, other global beer brands have added 3.2 billion dollars in market value.

Like buttoning a vest and missing a button hole, beer lovers knew something was not right with this risky campaign. CEO Brian Cornell defended the marketing strategy noting, "it was the right thing for society."

If it was so right, why has the company recently tried to ply the customer with "All-American" ads of flags and other patriotic symbols. If it was the right thing to do, why were the two ad executives placed on leave in the aftermath of the Mulvaney fiasco? If it was the right thing to do, why has the company made a $100 million promotional deal with the UFC (Ultimate Fighting Championship)?

About this same time, as the Bud Light controversy, Target rolled out a "PRIDE" collection featuring LGBTQ+ friendly clothing to *children*. Once again backlash devastated market values of the Minneapolis-based retailer. Consumers called for a boycott. It is reported that some even went into their local Target stores and tipped over displays of this line of clothing. It took only one week for Target to lose 9 billion dollars in market value.

You might find it interesting that these LGBTQ+ clothing and accessories are the creation of Abprallen, a London-based company that designs and sells occult and satanic-themed clothing to this subculture of deviants and naïve children.

Tomi Lahren, a conservative commentator, has said that Target is about to see its business suffer the same way that Bud Light did. She said, "Target…is about to get Bud Light-ed."

Retailers can insult their customer base with their woke values if they want. But they do so at their peril.

There is an old saying, "when you are in a hole, stop digging."

Anheuser-Busch and Target are relearning the art of merchandising. The same education could be in store for North Face clothing. They are feeling the heat of boycotts by consumers who are criticizing a recent roll out of advertising utilizing environmental activist Wyn Wiley, better known as drag queen, Pattie Gonia.

A firebrand member of Congress has encouraged consumers saying, "They can save a fortune not wasting money on labels that are grooming our children."

Depravity means we are bad and getting worse. Is there any hope for our nation?

Looking for Real Solutions

The Bible describes a *seared conscience* in 1 Timothy 4:2. The "conscience" is the God-given moral compass within each of us. Paul describes this kind of morality when writing to Roman believers noting, *They show that the work of the law is written on their hearts, while their conscience also bears witness...*(Romans 2:15)

When the conscience is *seared* (literally, cauterized), it has been rendered insensitive. Such a conscience does not work correctly. Like scar tissue is to our bodies, a *seared conscience* dulls the sense of right and wrong. Our moral compass no longer registers.

Obviously, our culture is guilty of having a *seared conscience*. However, even pagans recognize some levels of right and wrong. We know instinctively that some things are wrong. Children are off limits for most cultures. We do not need an eleventh commandment to instruct us in this matter. It is recognized that children are to be protected while they are developing. But for the perverted, children are the targets.

At the recent New York City's drag march, the chant, "We're here, we're queer, we're coming for your children," could be heard. It came to attention after a reporter affiliated with Timcast News reported the event. It lit parents across the nation aflame.

In defense, NBC responded, "The 'coming for your children' chant has been used for years at Pride events, according to longtime march attendees and gay rights activists, who said it's one of many provocative expressions used to regain control of slurs against LGBTQ+ people. And in this case, they said, right-wing activists are jumping on a single video to weaponize an out-of-context remark to further stigmatize the queer community."

Let's get this right—the chant has been used for years. Across the nation events such as drag shows, drag brunches, drag queen story hours in public libraries, LGBTQ+ PRIDE parades fill main streets. These are being used to target children. And those children's questionable parents are allowing this and promoting these events. This sounds like a long-term strategy to foster perversion in young, impressionable minds. When they say, "We're coming for your children," believe them.

When a fallen culture takes a bold stand against perversions advocated by beer companies and clothing outlets, maybe it signals a glimmer of hope for our culture. Their sensitivity and backlash to this social experimentation is a clear picture of a canary in a corrupt mine shaft.

The questions beg, "Where are the people of God in the midst of such cultural corruption? Has the Christian community lost or surrendered its influence in our culture?"

Leviticus 5:1 declares, *"If anyone sins in that he hears a public adjuration to testify, and though he is a witness, whether he has seen or come to know the matter, yet does not speak, he shall bear his iniquity."*

Keith Green, a pioneer of contemporary Christian music, said, "The world is asleep in darkness and the church is asleep in the light."

Oh, the need for canaries in our country has never been greater. Yet, the contemporary church is asleep while our culture rots before our sanctified eyes.

The symbol the LGBTQ+ coalition has taken is a rainbow. After the Flood, God placed a rainbow in the sky as a promise that He would not judge the world with water again. Wickedness has stolen this biblical symbol and it's time for the church to reclaim it.

Is it possible? Yes. There is hope for America when Christian canaries unite in petitioning the Lord for a heaven-sent, sin-killing, God-honoring revival and spiritual awakening. It begins with a call to repentance.

The call for personal and national repentance

The power of incremental change is tremendous. Rarely do we have dramatic, life-altering changes in our lives. This is true whether it is dealing with learning something new or losing that excess weight. Isaiah described the process of incrementalism: *For it is precept upon precept, precept upon precept, line upon line, line upon line, here a little, there a little* (Is. 28:10). As teaching young children, great changes develop through incremental development of knowledge.

While great change comes through incremental steps, true spiritual change begins with one essential, initial change. The Bible describes that supernatural change as "repentance."

The English term "repent" flows from two Greek words. One is *metaniono* and translates as "regret." It is *to express sorrow*. Turn on a television news broadcast and observe a report that highlights a criminal who has been apprehended by authorities. Sometimes, this culprit hides behind a jacket or sweater during his perp walk. This is a picture of *metaniono*. This individual "regrets" he or she has been caught. However, this person has no intention of changing behavior.

It is also called, "legal repentance." That form of regret occurs on interstate highways regularly. A driver knowingly exceeds the speed limit—until he sees a state trooper. What happens next? He taps the brakes just enough to slow down. As soon as the coast is clear, the driver speeds up again. Legal repentance is regret. But that driver will choose to speed again.

"Repent" utilizes a second Greek term. *Metano* is a verb that means, "to change one's mind." This kind of repentance is detailed in the relationship of national Israel to God.

The Hebrews had made a covenant with Jehovah at Mount Sinai (Ex. 19). God warned them of turning to idols and false Gods when they came into the land He had promised them. *Then it shall come about when the LORD your God brings you into the land which He swore to your fathers, Abraham, Isaac and Jacob, to give you, great and splendid cities which you did not build, and houses full of all good things which you did not fill, and hewn cisterns which you did not dig, vineyards and olive trees which you did not plant, and you shall eat and be satisfied, then watch yourself, lest you forget the LORD who brought you from the land of Egypt, out of the house of slavery...You shall not follow other gods, any of the gods of the peoples who surround you* (Dt. 6:10-12, 14 NASB).

Again and again, the nation went through the faithful/faithless cycle. The book of Judges, as we mentioned earlier, details this cycle. The messages of the prophets were primarily calls for Israel's repentance. They implored the nation, the people of God, to return to Him. That return was repentance.

As the emphasis shifted to a new covenant, individuals were called to repentance. Both nation and person were called to repent—*"Therefore I will judge you, O house of Israel, each according to his conduct," declares the Lord GOD. "**Repent and turn away** from all your transgressions, so that iniquity may not become a stumbling block to you. "Cast away from you all your transgressions which you have committed, and make yourselves a new heart and a new spirit! For why will you die, O house of Israel? For I have no pleasure in the death of anyone who dies," declares the Lord GOD. "Therefore, repent and live"* (Ezek. 18:30-32 NASB).

We are nearing a dangerous time as a culture. The bleak winds of destiny are howling in protest to the way we are living. The hope America has today is found in responding to a biblical call to "change our minds" about the condition of our nation in free-fall. It demands national and individual repentance.

That's you and me. Genuine repentance will touch my house, your house, and the White House.

The crisis is real. The time is short. The choice is clear. It's time to return to unwavering devotion to the Lord.

Personal Repentance

What might that look like? Imagine drawing a circle on the ground. Personal repentance begins by stepping inside that circle and asking the Lord to change everyone in that circle...that's you. Repentance is an initial step to cleanse us of wicked ways. Sins of commission (actions we do) and sins of omission (actions we should do but don't) will likely be included in this spiritual cleansing.

Maybe you have never placed your trust in Jesus as Savior and Lord. The call is to "change your mind" —about ourselves, about our sin, about Him. We are not God. Our rebellion has separated us from God. Jesus died for our sins, was raised for our justification, and He is Lord. One day all humanity will stand before Him to give an account for our lives. Are you ready for that Day?

You can be by simply admitting your sin (confess), change your mind about yourself, your sin, and God (repentance) and believe that Christ died for you and was raised from the dead (faith), God will save you. Romans 10:9-10, 13 affirms that promise: *because, if you confess with your mouth that Jesus is Lord and believe in your heart that God raised him from the dead, you will be saved. For with the heart one believes and is justified, and with the mouth one confesses and is saved...For "everyone who calls on the name of the Lord will be saved."*

Someone has said that "the only problem with a living sacrifice is that it tends to crawl off the altar." Like Israel, we are prone to wander. We stray from the path of righteousness. Therefore, daily examination and attendant repentance is necessary to be in close fellowship with our Father. Repentance is, therefore, an initial step to relationship and a necessary discipline of fellowship.

How are we doing in our walk with the Lord? Straying or staying close? Closeness is only a prayer away.

National Repentance

The account of the reluctant prophet Jonah is an account of national repentance. Jonah was sent to the Assyrian Empire, the second great empire of the Mesopotamian Valley. When the delinquent prophet traveled through the capital city of Nineveh, he preached repentance to every person. Look at the response:

The word reached the king of Nineveh, and he arose from his throne, removed his robe, covered himself with sackcloth, and sat in ashes. And he issued a proclamation and published through Nineveh, "By the decree of the king and his nobles: Let neither man nor beast, herd nor flock, taste anything. Let them not feed or drink water, but let man and beast be covered with sackcloth, and let them call out mightily to God. Let everyone turn from his evil way and from the violence that is in his hands. Who knows? God may turn and relent and turn from his fierce anger, so that we may not perish (Jonah 3:6-9."

The nation—the whole nation, king to kids, even to the beasts—repented in sackcloth and ashes. Sackcloth and ashes were an outward sign of mourning, repentance, submission, or abasement. The ashes were a sign signaling to everyone absolute grief, desolation, and ruin. Because of their repentance, the life of their empire was extended.

Maybe it is time for some sackcloth and ashes in America.

Nehemiah 1:6-10 is also a national call to repentance. Nehemiah's heartfelt brokenness over the destruction of Jerusalem's protective walls drove him to move a nation to change by returning to the Lord:

...let your ear be attentive and your eyes open, to hear the prayer of your servant that I now pray before you day and night for the people of Israel your servants, confessing the sins of the people of Israel, which we have sinned against you. Even I and my father's house have sinned. We have acted very corruptly against you and have not kept the commandments, the statutes, and the rules that you commanded your servant Moses. Remember the word that you commanded your servant Moses, saying, 'If you are unfaithful, I will scatter you among the peoples, but if you return to me and keep my commandments and do them, though your outcasts are in the uttermost parts of heaven, from there I will gather them and bring them to the place that I have chosen, to make my name dwell there.' They

213

are your servants and your people, whom you have redeemed by your great power and by your strong hand.

In the prayer of Nehemiah, we hear the anguish of the soul. The sorrow over and the ownership of sin against God. But in that prayer is the promise of restoration if repentance and return are done.

Psalm 33:12 is a powerful promise to every broken generation past and present: *Blessed is the nation whose God is the LORD...*

Biblical canaries are warning our culture for the need for personal and national repentance. Pleading for us to return to the Lord.

The call for renewal and spiritual awakening

The Lord's faithful words are a clarion call for revival among His people. We have the promise of God, *if my people who are called by my name humble themselves, and pray and seek my face and turn from their wicked ways, then I will hear from heaven and will forgive their sin and heal their land* (2 Chronicles 7:14). This is a conditional promise. The conditions are clearly seen:

- *if my people*—not the heathen, but rather, the people of God
- *humble themselves*—humility, not PRIDE is the requirement
- *and pray*—seek God praying in the power of the Holy Spirit
- *and seek my face*—seek His face, not His hand for blessing
- *and turn*—this is the essential turning away, turning around
- *then I will hear*—when conditions are met, God listens
- *will forgive*—God will "send away" our sin
- *will heal their land*—the cure is in relationship with God

The English word "revive" flows from Latin terminology meaning, "life again." For there to be "life again," means there was life somewhere in the past. God is eager to manifest His reviving presence and power to our generation. But it means we must take necessary steps to release His sanctifying power in our lives.

The greatest need in the lives of the people of God, the called-

214

out-ones, is to be the best possible ambassadors of righteousness for a culture in crisis. An ambassador is the highest ranking representative of one government or kingdom to another. As the people of God, we are His ambassadors (2 Cor. 5:20). We need awakened individuals to influence our nation to the core of its being. When God's people choose holiness, a corrupt culture will be challenged with the gospel of God's redemption.

Let us test and examine our ways and return to the Lord!

Lamentations 3:40

Spiritual revivals are rare in our country. A tutorial about revival characteristics is essential in today's church. Understanding the nature of revival and cooperating where God is working allows fresh winds to continue without being impeded. Revival surges in and through the church. According to Leonard Ravenhill, revival is fueled by prayer. He says, "God's doesn't answer prayer. He answers desperate prayer!" Revival is birthed in prevailing prayer.

When will the body of Christ become so desperate about the decay of our culture that we are driven to prevailing prayer? When will believers shake off indifference, apathy, and unconcern? When conditions for revival are met by God's people, then we will see Him move in our midst.

What happens when we experience true revival?

Sin is exposed.

Generally, revival is preceded by a Laodicean syndrome. Defections by nominal believers is normal. Dullness and lethargy envelope God's people. Darkness settles inside the church.

When revival comes, brokenness will be the order of the day. God's people become sensitive to His power. In Isaiah-like-fashion we confess, *"Woe is me! ... for I am a man of unclean lips, and I dwell in the midst of a people of unclean lips."*

The deeper sin is confessed, the deeper a saint is cleansed.

Opposition explodes.

When revival comes, we should expect conflict from two sources. Obviously, we will be opposed by the forces of darkness. Also, apathy will be challenged among members of the household of faith. We should not be surprised when marginal believers rise up against God's divine moment. When Nehemiah came to Jerusalem to rebuild the wall, he was opposed from within and from without.

The Apostle Paul noted that the experiences recorded in the Old Testament are examples for us as the people of God (1 Cor. 10:6). The example of Nehemiah forewarns us of what to expect. We enter the battle for the nation with the expectation of opposition from without and from within.

Strongholds implode.

When revival comes, marriages are healed and families reunited. Churches will enjoy unity instead of division. Revival cleanses the body of Christ of her strongholds. Freedom from sin's shackles finally comes. God-sent sentinels who desperately pray are pivotal.

Revival is the cure for a needy church. Spiritual awakening is the cure for a needy culture. What is a spiritual awakening? It's just that! It occurs when a spiritually sleeping culture is awakened by the power of God. Spiritual awakening is when the Holy Spirit moves in a heart, home, town, or region. This divine moment spreads like a forest wildfire. Dynamic and noticeable changes toward the things of the Lord are instantaneous.

Spiritual awakenings are an important element of our American heritage. The First Great Awakening occurred between the 1730 and 1770. It was in some ways a stimulus for the Revolution in America encouraging the ideas of liberty, equality, and self-reliance.

Then came the Second Great Awakening sweeping across the landscape of American culture from 1790 to decades into the 1800s. God baptized the new nation of the United States in the flame of the Holy Spirit. Revival and evangelistic fires spread across the cities, towns, and even into the frontier settlements. So many were converted in upper New York and Canada, that areas were dubbed "Burned-Over Districts." The spiritual fervor was so high in these regions that it seemed to set the places on fire.

Spiritual awakening is a special work of the Holy Spirit among people as He creates an unusual awareness and openness to Jesus Christ. In these spiritual awakenings, the lost are saved and the saved are revived. They had effects on the personal lives of individuals and on the public life of the nation. It's beyond time for another awakening to occur.

Oh Lord please raise up an army of intercessors who will "stand in the gap" for our culture.

In 1927, a USS S-4 submarine of the United States Navy sunk after being struck by another ship. The trapped men used the last available oxygen in the sub to send a morse-coded message that read, *"Is there any hope?"*

Forty sailors died in that watery coffin a mile off Provincetown, Massachusetts' shoreline.

But their question remains for our nation today. Is there any hope? With every confidence, many canaries crisscrossing our nation would shout, "YES." But the solution is a repentant people who have experienced a special work of the Holy Spirit called revival and spiritual awakening.

Conclusion

It is not possible nor plausible for anyone to assume that revival will be experienced by *everyone.* No. Such uniformity will not occur in any other nation. It will not occur in America either. However, our culture can be influenced as a greater number of people like you and me return to the Lord. Past generations have experienced that transformation. It is time for this generation to press into the things of the Lord with irresistible passion to know Him and to make Him known. We can influence this culture in free fall for His glory.

Jesus described believers of every generation as salt and light. Like salt enhances the flavor of food, our faithfulness flavors our culture and creates thirst for the Lord. Like light penetrates darkness, our lives are to penetrate a corrupt culture and expose them to the Light of the world—Jesus.

The prayer for the message of *A Canary in a Coal Mine* is to stir every reader deeply enough to become engaged. How?

Be willing to engage the culture with a righteous indignation. *"Be angry,"* Paul says, *"but do not sin."* Every concerned believer has a reason of hope within them that must be shared graciously but without compromise.

Fellow canary, observing how quickly our culture is collapsing should stir us so deeply that it propels us into the marketplace of thought as well as the voting booth.

Be broken-hearted over the spiritual darkness that envelops our culture. Paul describes the beginning steps on the downward spiral of humanity like this: *For although they knew God, they did not honor him as God or give thanks to him, but they became futile in their thinking, and their foolish hearts were darkened. Claiming to be wise, they became fools, and exchanged the glory of the immortal God for images resembling mortal man and birds and animals and creeping things* (Romans 1:21-23).

Such is the path of this declining culture. It is feared the spiritual darkness our nation endures is because bad people do bad things and godly people do nothing!

Grieve over our dying culture. What we know should give sleepless nights to millions of believers in Jesus Christ. This burden should not be relieved until pointed actions are taken to "stand in the gap" for our nation.

The hymn, *Stand Up, Stand Up for Jesus*, was written in 1858 by George Duffield. Due to the language of the day, the third stanza of the hymn has an interesting turn of phrase:

Stand up, stand up for Jesus, stand in his strength alone;
the arm of flesh will fail you, ye dare not trust your own.
Put on the gospel armor, each piece put on with prayer;
where duty calls or danger, ***be never wanting there***.

That last line always confused me as we sang this song in a small rural church a lifetime ago. The stanza reflects the spiritual warfare Paul described in his Ephesian letter. The call of the epistle and this hymn is to spiritual battle. But the line states—"be never wanting there." The question always ran through my mind as a child, "Who wants to be in war anyway?" But that was not the meaning of that word, *wanting*. It is an older use for "do not be missing."

The image comes from the experience of Gideon who commanded his 300 warriors to stand around the camp of the enemy. Armed with only horns, empty jars, and torches, the army of Gideon put to flight the enemy army. Why? Because each man was in his place. The impression created was that the enemy was completely surrounded. Had any man "been wanting" in his place, the battle would have been lost. However, because no gap was in the line, victory was theirs.

Because each man stood his ground, the enemy had no place to hide. Confused and frightened, the Midianites were defeated and never returned to inflict suffering on God's people.

Stand up. We live out of our feelings. Like you, many other sentinels have developed a steely-eyed stare with a passion that motivates us to engage in the battle for the nation. The outcome will affect the future of generations to come.

James, the half-brother of Jesus, described this kind of passion when he said, *Be doers of the word and not hearers only* (James 1:22).

The English word "hearers" comes from a root Greek term, *akon,* and carries the idea of auditing a class in college. Like an auditing student who has no reason to master the discipline of a certain course, believers are commanded not merely to audit their faith.

It's time to get into the fray. It's past time for a canary like you to move. Recall the estimates that approximately 30 million believers chose not to vote in the 2012 presidential election. And 6 - 7% of evangelical voters chose to sit on their ballots rather than cast them in the 2020 election. Look what we got. Look where we are. We are not to be "wanting." We cannot afford to sit it out.

The 2024 through 2028 election cycles are the most important maybe in our lifetimes. For the moment, let's set aside the "R" and "D" and consider becoming purple patriots.

Voting is a privilege and a requirement under our system of government. It demands responsible and careful consideration of the platforms of all candidates. If you are still foggy about voting, why not use God's Word as a filter for the flood of information you will receive. Allow your vote to be cast for the person whom you feel has the hand of the Lord upon them. Honestly, the choice is becoming clearer by the day.

Will you be a canary in 2024? May the wisdom of Solomon wash over the heart and life of every canary who dares to be a sentinel in these desperate but promising days.

Recall the primary requirement of a steward: *Moreover, it is required of stewards that they be found faithful* (1 Cor. 4:2). We have a stewardship in our country for liberty.

Fellow canary…let's be faithful!

Lutheran pastor and theologian, Martin Niemöller, was born in Germany in 1892. His public addresses in the 1930's were born from a concern that his country was going off the rails. Demented leadership was filling the German government which was struggling in the aftermath of World War I. Germany was being seized systematically by a Nationalist Party known as Nazis. Niemöller's musings almost 100 years ago, mirror the miseries our nation faces today.

"First, they came…"

First they came for the Socialists, and I did not speak out—because I was not a Socialist.
Then they came for the Trade Unionists, and I did not speak out—because I was not a Trade Unionist.
Then they came for the Jews, and I did not speak out—because I was not a Jew.
Then they came for me—and there was no one left to speak for me.

His reflections are a warning to us. We cannot be silent. We cannot be still. *Carpe diem*, seize the day. If we do not heed Niemöller's warning, the moment will be gone and we will pass into a dark future. The horrors of which we cannot fathom.

But we have the moment now, what shall we do?

Every canary needs to be equipped for the future.

Has our culture gone over the edge? Have we reached the point of no return? That's debatable. For the moment, let's not throw in the towel on America. Let's unite in turning back the tide of corruption that rages in the Beltway. How? Here are three steps to consider:

Step # 1 – Information

Information is power. Gather information. Become a student of American culture. Did you know that an expert is someone who invests only 1000 hours on any discipline? The more a canary knows the better decision making will occur. This is not a time to stick our collective heads in the sand. It's time to stick our necks out with the same passionate determination that our forefathers had. Let's create a flock of experts in the coming days.

The enemies and challenges we face are from the center to the circumference and all around the circumference. Internal and external enemies seek to destroy our nation. The angles of attack are so many that they boggle the mind. It is easy to be overwhelmed.

Absorb what you can. Focus on a few key issues. For you, it might be only one issue. It might be election integrity. It might be the assault on our children by the indoctrination pods called schools. It might be the national debt. Whatever the cause that rings your bell might just be the call of God. The passion and concern you have might very well be the place where God wants you to be engaged. That might be your place on the battle line.

Step # 2 - Transformation

We should not settle for simply being armed with information about our culture. Digesting information correlates with changed behavior. Paul described the power of transformation when writing in Romans 12:1-2—

I appeal to you therefore, brothers, by the mercies of God, to present your bodies as a living sacrifice, holy and acceptable to God, which is your spiritual worship.

He continues,

Do not be conformed to this world, but be transformed by the renewing of your mind, that by testing you may discern what is that will of God, what is good and acceptable and perfect.

How does a believer experience transformation? By fostering a renewing mindset. That comes through a consistent fellowship with God and feeding on the sole authority of His word, the Bible. Two key words jump off the page to every believer. "Conformed," is the Greek term, *schematizo*. It carries the idea of assuming an outward expression that does not originate from within. The imagery is of being pressed into a mold. The outward form produced by being pressed into the mold of the world is not representative of the changed inner person of a believer in Jesus Christ.

But, he urges, be *metamorphoomai*, or "transformed" by the renewing of your thinking. This term reminds us of elementary lessons in science. Butterflies have no resemblance to the caterpillar; tad poles have no resemblance to frogs. Like these two creatures experience metamorphosis, so too are believers to be transformed. In a transformed state, we evaluate our culture through the filters of the Bible.

Transformed individuals transform a nation.

Step # 3 – Perspiration

Returning our culture to "one nation under God..." will demand work. It will involve a willingness of every canary to influence their relational circles. Imagine you are casting a stone into a calm body of water. A ripple effect is created. The point of entry by the stone is the most dramatic. Though less dramatic and noticeable, every molecule of water in that body is influenced by that stone.

Fellow canary, you have influence. Use it! Start with your immediate family; then move to extended family; from there touch neighbors, work associates, and businesses you frequent. You might encounter divine appointments with perfect strangers.

Influence can happen in large groups. However, often people can be lost in the shuffle of any large organization. Influence can be minimized. A wise canary understands that influence spreads faster and deeper in small groups. Even in one-to-one encounters. Imagine what could happen if a political icon became an army of canaries? The message spreading father to son, mother to daughter, friend to friend, neighbor to neighbor, associate to associate. This was what caused the early Christian faith to spread like wildfire over the Roman Empire. Within three centuries the whole Empire was changed—slave to sovereign called Christ, "Lord."

Changing our culture will demand such an army. Fellow canaries, we can challenge our culture to change. Elections are coming upon us soon. We should move quickly and precisely to keep from being run over by the business-as-usual corrupt politics.

How do we effect change?

Pray for our culture.   Prayer gains divine attention. The eyes of the Lord are searching for canaries across our land who are willing to allow God to prove Himself strong.   Please petition the Lord for healing in our land.

Participant in change. Begin with local government. Learn how it works (or doesn't). Consider deepening your walk by being informed of statewide processes and issues. Then, be fearless in addressing the "kick-the can-down-the-road" mindset that plagues our federal government.

That story of Gideon is a clear picture of fearlessly standing in the face of opposition. God used Gideon to rid the nation of their enemies, the Midianites. Surely, God's way for turning a nation is unique. Here is a man who started with 32,000 volunteers for an army. The Lord led Gideon to chop his military force to a mere 300 men. They were the human instruments in the hands of the Lord.

From 32,000 down to 300. A reduction of force by 99%. That wasn't much of a force. But it was enough in God's hands.

"History is written by the 1%," said G. Edward Griffin. "These are the idea creators and shapers. The 1% affects 3% who are activists. These are the ones who make things happen. These affect another 11% who are the doers. These are the ones who decide to do something about the situation. This 15% can change the world."

This is in line with the quip, "The world is filled with three groups of people: those who make it happen; those who watch it happen; and those who don't know what happened."

Our failing culture desperately needs believers to take a stand. Let's find our place and stand too? Let's be found faithful as Paul commanded, *Endure hardness as a good soldier* for Jesus.

Stay engaged until change comes. The unrelenting, long-term strategy of those who choose a deviant lifestyle illustrates this. Our culture did not get in the shape it is in overnight; it will take time to recover from our personal and national sin. It might take generations to be engaged in needed changes in our federal government.

There is a difference between a squash plant and an oak tree. A squash is around for a few days. A mighty oak requires years. But the strength of the oak endures. Be strong, be faithful, be a canary in this cultural coal mine.

Christian canary, the time to get outside the salt box called a church is overdue. If we do not act now, America as we have known it is over.

Remember what is affirmed throughout Scripture and history: God establishes kingdoms and sets their parameters. In His transcendence and omniscience, He causes empires and nations to rise and fall. God determines the times and seasons of nations and governments. His will ultimately prevails.

As His followers, we have the duty to be good citizens. Now. Where we are. Under the temporal kingdom in which we reside. Praying for our leaders. Submitting to the laws that govern us. America is not a tyranny like the Roman Empire. We are a Republic. We are to be subject to the government. *And in America, we are the government.*

The question of our time, of our nation, and in our lives is—will we be obedient? In our system of government, we must participate. Few nations have had such a structure. It is a privilege that carries responsibility.

Let us not be found wanting. Arise!

Steps to take now:

Action # 1: Do a personal study on the First and Second Great Awakenings.

Action # 2: Do a personal study or interview someone who was a part of the revival at Asbury College in Wilmore, KY. The most recent movement of God occurred in 2022.

Action # 3: Perform a personal confession season and come clean before the Lord.   Repent of any thoughts or actions that keep you from obedience and fellowship with God.

Action # 4: Jesus told His disciples that some circumstances can only be addressed by prayer and fasting (Mark 9:29). Consider establishing the discipline of prayer and fasting to address the monumental crises facing our nation. Pray for our nation to turn again to the Lord seeking His will, glory, and blessing on America.

Action # 5: Identify the two or three issues that are of highest concern for you. Seek information on these issues. Connect with others who share the same concerns. Determine how you can be engaged in addressing these issues.

Epilogue

Their story is saturated with triumph and tragedy. Bob Mays and Jim Stone were childhood friends who lived in a small mining town in the heart of the Alleghany Mountains. Coal mining was in their blood. Their grandfathers and fathers were coal miners and entering the bowels of the earth in search of another vein of black gold was their destiny as well. It's what they knew.

Some rare exceptions came when young men escaped the horrors of coal mining by receiving scholarships to play college athletics. That was not the case for Bob Mays and Jim Stone. Like so many others, these two friends knew they would enter the coal mine as young men only to exit as broken old men.

Graduation from high school was an exciting time for these two friends. However, a cloud of reality settled over them as the day approached for them to don cover-alls, steel-toed boots, and a flashlight attached to a silver miner's cap.

Young men learned the business of coal mining from seasoned veterans who knew a coal mine shaft like the back of their hands. Bob and Jim were no exceptions. The education was quick, simple, and direct. Either they learned how to make a living and survive to tell the story or they would be listed in the obituary section of their local paper.

One vivid lesson of their initiation into coal mining was to appreciate the work of canaries in cages that were present in every mining shaft. However, these two friends brushed off the reasons why these little birds were partners in the routine of digging coal. Years passed for Bob and Jim. Marriage came and then children along with customary revolving debt at the local company stores.

They became professional coal miners who were admired by other workers because of their ability to extract record amounts of coal. All the while, those little birds became companions in their work. Canaries became so familiar that these two friends developed a sense of being invulnerable to the dangers of their hazardous job. Bob and Jim began taking unnecessary risks by venturing deeper into a darkness where death awaited the unaware.

Soon a day came when shining a light on the cavern ceiling, Jim shouted, "Hey Bob, I think we have found the mother lode!"

Both men were excited that this single vein could possibly meet the weekly quota of production. Then, the years of training reminded Bob of the importance of having a canary in a coal mine. Jim was already working the vein.

Bob said to Jim who was already shoring up the shaft, "I'm going to get the bird, Jim."

Only a few minutes passed before Bob returned with their little sentinel.

Both friends were swinging their picks as coal fell at their feet unlike any time in their lives. Then, as Bob was adjusting the light on his cap, he caught a glimpse of their companion bird. It was twitching…thrashing inside the cage. He tapped Jim on the back while pointing to the canary.

"Jim, it's time to get out of here," he exclaimed. But Jim kept on working all the while ignoring the warning of the canary. "Jim, it's time to go NOW!"

Jim said, "I've got time to load the cart with this coal." He said, "Bob, you go on and I will be right behind you."

By now, the canary was motionless. Bob begged his lifelong friend to move quickly. But to no avail. For some reason,

Jim remained at the task ignoring the pleas of his friend and a dead canary in a cage.

Becoming more light-headed by the moment, Bob began making his way to safety. His search for fresh air and safety came with the reality that Jim had not followed him out of the mine shaft. About an hour passed before rescue teams arrived on scene to locate the lone miner. They found Jim unresponsive, slumped over a half-full cart of coal and clutching the cage of a lifeless bird.

The obituary for Jim Stone recorded a brief summary of his life. His surviving wife and grieving children were listed along with extended family. Accolades about him were extended from across the small mining community. His life-long friend Bob was given the privilege of eulogizing his comrade.

When his opportunity came to speak, Bob stood up before the grieving audience. His voice was shaky and cracking. After a lengthy pause, he said, "We are here today to say 'goodbye' to a father, husband, co-worker, and my best friend."

After a few brief words, Bob stated, "If only Jim would have listened to my warning. If only Jim would have heeded the warning of that little canary!" Bob lowered his head and said, "Jim would be with us today."

"There was no reason for him to die at this early age in life. He died too young."

The eulogy continued, "Jim had every opportunity to escape the chamber of death that took his life." He groaned, "Oh, how I will miss my friend. I will be haunted with his memory for the rest of my life because I did not convince him of the deadly situation, we both faced that day."

Bob's closing words pierced the heart every coal miner and family present that day. "If only Jim had paid attention to the canary in the coal mine."

Appendix

I once had a friend who took me rabbit hunting. We packed everything needed for the day including lunch, shotguns, and four beagles. Along the way, he told me that beagles will snip and bite each other in their cages. However, once these dogs are released in the hunt, a transformation occurs. These animals passionately focus on rabbits. When these dogs find the scent, it is a sight to watch them execute their training. Once on the scent, they find the trail.

A Canary in a Coal Mine is designed to help purple patriots "find the scent" of cultural failures that touch their lives and then, become active in doing something about changing it, making it better, strengthening it, or in some cases stand against the swelling tide these failures ultimately bring to communities across the nation. Here are a few ways—an Action Plan—to become a "canary" in your community.

EDUCATE – Be informed!

- Christians should immerse themselves in the Word of God. Before we are informed politically, we need to be informed biblically. Our intent has been to address the crucial cultural threats to our nation from a biblical, theological perspective. You might begin your informed opinion with the Scripture references that are referred to in this text.

- Narrow your focus. What concerns you about our nation in free fall? There are avenues to address your concerns:
  ⇒ National concerns – Meet your Congressional representatives. Take them to lunch and build a relationship with them. Guard against being adversarial. Try to befriend them. These politicians are people just like you. Gather their contact information: phone, email, texting, and so forth.

Let them know that you are there to help them solve the issues that concern you. To inform them of your concerns, after all, they represent you. If they know how you feel or think about certain issues, it will help them represent your concerns better. It gives them authority when they stand to speak and act on your behalf.

⇒ State concerns – This audience will be a bit easier to attain. Though busy, these elected officials are most likely to be accessible to meeting with you.

⇒ Local concerns – These are your neighbors and friends. Conversations seem to be easier with people we know and who know us.

- Be sure of your facts. That will demand learning how to research the issue of concern and becoming conversant about it. Discover the voting record of your representative and challenge them in areas in which you might not agree with their voting. List reasons why. Consider their voting record and actions. Go beyond and behind the rhetoric. Many can talk a good game. But their record is their record. When elections come, gain as much information as possible. We might not find that person who aligns with our every value and policy position. But we can find that person who more nearly aligns with our Christian values and world view in their policies and actions.

- Be an advocate for your concerns. Offer to help your representative discover solutions to the concerns being discussed. Agree to disagree with them but be kind. A firm position does not have to be clothed in anger. Before the meeting concludes, ask for clarifications of the issues discussed, for steps the representative will consider, and for a follow up meeting to evaluate progress toward solutions.

- Identify the 2 or 3 issues that draw your passion. It is easy to feel overwhelmed because of the multitude of issues facing us. Narrow your focus on the issues key to you. Others will be called to address other issues. The result will be that we collectively address the key issues that will correct the course and preserve the nation.

- Seek sources that will help you understand the issues and the governmental policies that can be or are being formulated to address the issues with action. For instance, the America First Policy Institute does just this. Only recently at a townhall meeting did we become aware of the AFPI's work. We were in the final stages of writing this book. We checked them out and offer their contact as a place to begin educating yourself on many key issues. This information might help you formulate a personal action plan. Check them out at—https://americafirstpolicy.com.

  However, these policies (or those from other sources of information) must be measured against the Word of God and your faith. Process your thinking with other Christian friends, with your pastor, or with other Christian leaders across the country.

ENGAGE – Connect with your representatives.

- Pray. For yourself. For our government representatives. This aligns us with God in obedience.

- Schedule routine encounters with your representatives. Invite them to lunch. Attend townhall meetings. Travel to where they are meeting and make your presence known.

- Send thank you cards, Christmas cards, special occasion cards. Help them recognize you as an advocate not an adversary.

- Offer to work their re-election campaign in the future. Ask them to mentor you in becoming a candidate for office too. For example, consider running for open positions on your local school board. The representative you have befriended can be a major source of encouragement in championing your campaign.

- Pray for supernatural insight to be given. Whether voting for a candidate or running for office, seek the Lord's direction as you move closer to election day.

- Create a voter registration center in your church.

- Provide information on issues and candidates.

- Conduct a voter registration/community canvass. As Christian citizens, we are encouraging every citizen to vote.

ENLIST – Influence your circles of influence.

- Enlist others in your circle to join you in consistent prayer. Enlarge that circle seeking the will of God for our nation.

- Encourage your immediate and extended family to strongly consider your candidate in an upcoming election. Talk with your neighbors and co-workers about your experiences with the candidate. Be a voice of affirmation to those you influence. Do not assume your circles of influence know about the candidate (s). Help them to see voting records and how our representatives' voting records affect outcomes and decision making.

- Express values not opinions. Values are those items that strengthen communities and culture. For example, rather than complaining about teenage crime, discover ways to influence these young men and women to becoming valuable citizens.

These are simple suggestions for your consideration. You can make a plan that fits your needs and lifestyle. The keys are to educate, engage, and enlist!

Addendum 1

The America First Policy Institute

AFPI is pursuing a robust policy agenda that puts America First and its people first. These policies are broken down into ten thematic pillars subdivided into specific policy centers, which drive towards the mission of putting the American people first.

Look at their web site to find detailed information on policies that affect your lives and our nation.

https://americafirstpolicy.com

Here is a sample of the Areas of Interest you can explore:

International Affairs
Environment
Healthcare
Immigration
Media Bias
Social Issues and Values
Election Integrity
Criminal Justice Reform
Censorship
Critical Race Theory
Energy
Security
Economy
International Trade
Education

Ten Pillars
1. Make the Greatest Economy in the World Work for All
   Americans

2. Put Patients and Doctors in Charge of Healthcare
3. Restore American Historic Commitment to Freedom, Equality, and Self-governance
4. Give Parents Control Over Education of Their Children
5. Finish the Wall, End Human Trafficking, and Defeat Drug Cartels
6. Deliver Peace through Strength and American Leadership
7. Make America Energy Independent
8. Make it Easy to Vote and Hard to Cheat
9. Provide Safe and Secure Communities so all Americans Can Live Their Lives in Peace
10. Fight Government Corruption by Draining the Swamp

Biblical Foundations for America First Policy Institution

The idea of mixing religion and public discourse has been made into an untouchable idea in the U.S., but in reality, God has called His Church to be active in the issues of our day. An accompanying sermon series will underline the biblical foundation for each of America First Policy Institute's 10 foundational pillars for America. Without the guidance of the Holy Bible in a world full of evil, it is impossible to safeguard the future of America for the next generation.

Our Christian and biblical values over the last two centuries matter. The extraordinary progress, prosperity, freedom, and equality it has produced matters. The Church in the U.S. must play a significant role in standing for the values and freedoms that have made America the most prosperous nation on Earth. This is not about building a state religion; it's about maintaining the country's foundational Judeo-Christian values that secured the Nation's future over the last two and half centuries.

Jesus has called His Church to participate in the marketplace of ideas actively. We are called to be the light of the world and the salt of the Earth. If the Church does not engage in the issues of the day, then it is missing a historic opportunity at a critical point in America's story to partner in bringing the kingdom of heaven to Earth. We must act. We must vote. We must run for public office. We must plant Jesus in every space we are allowed to stand while we are still allowed to stand and speak God's truth.

We must do this because, as we have seen in history that power corrupts, and absolute power corrupts absolutely. We are witnessing the progression of that every day in our government, our media, and our schools. Freedoms and liberties guaranteed in our Constitution are under assault. This fight is not just about the culture of America; it's about the kingdom of God and the Church's divine mission to be the salt and light of our day in an era of increasing darkness.

It is not too late for America. And it's not too late to surrender to the unshakable truth found in 2 Chronicles 7:14: *"If My people who are called by My name will humble themselves, and pray and seek My face, and turn from their wicked way, then I will hear from heaven, and will forgive their sin and heal their land."* The call to action is for God's people. Prayer is our first action, but it must be coupled with physical works. The book of James declares that faith without works is dead. Faith in action produces policy that stands the test of time and that honors God and his design for mankind through righteous governance. In other words, it is a governance that is under God, indivisible, that delivers liberty and justice for all.

To access more on the biblical foundations, go to the AFPI web site and enter in the Search prompt: Biblical Foundations. That will take you to the biblical and sermon resources offered by America First Policy Institute.

www.ingramcontent.com/pod-product-compliance
Lightning Source LLC
Chambersburg PA
CBHW062323120626
46553CB00015B/333